2 Copies not on list

TAKING MEASURES ACROSS THE AMERICAN LANDSCAPE

TAKING MEASURES

Across the American Landscape

James Corner
Essays, Drawings, and Commentary

Alex S. MacLean
Photographs

Foreword *by* Michael Van Valkenburgh

Yale University Press

New Haven and London

Published with assistance from the Graham Foundation for Advanced Studies in the Fine Arts
and from the University of Pennsylvania Research Foundation.

Designed by Lisa C. Tremaine.
Set in type by Highwood Typographic Services, Hamden, Connecticut.
Printed by C&C Offset Printing Co. Ltd. , Hong Kong.

Library of Congress Cataloging-in-Publications Data
Corner, James
    Taking measures across the American landscape / James Corner, essays, drawings, and
    commentary; Alex S. MacLean, photographs ; foreword by Michael Van Valkenburgh ; with an
    essay by Denis Cosgrove.
        p.   cm.
    Includes bibliographic references and index.
    ISBN 0-300-06566-3 (alk. paper)
    1. Landscape photography—United States.   2. United States—Pictorial works.   I. MacLean,
    Alex S.   II. Title.
    TR660.5.C67   1996   96-1557
    304.2′3′0973—dc20   CIP

A catalogue record for this book is available from the British Library.
The paper in this book meets the guidelines for permanence and durability of the Committee
on Production Guidelines for Book Longevity of the Council on Library Resources.
10 9 8 7 6 5 4 3 2

Frontispiece: *Citrus Groves with Sprinkler Irrigation* (detail). Blythe, California.

In my beginning is my end. . . .
. . . .
                              . . . Round and round the fire
Leaping through the flames, or joined in circles,
Rustically solemn or in rustic laughter
Lifting heavy feet in clumsy shoes,
Earth feet, loam feet, lifted in country mirth
Mirth of those long since under earth
Nourishing the corn. Keeping time,
Keeping the rhythm in their dancing
As in their living in the living seasons
The time of the seasons and the constellations
The time of milking and the time of harvest
The time of the coupling of man and woman
And that of beasts. Feet rising and falling.
Eating and drinking. Dung and death.
                              —T. S. ELIOT, "East Coker"

CONTENTS

FOREWORD

The contemporary American landscape is magical and, at times, beautiful. The collision and layering of the pieces of today's landscape, like fragments of our perplexing and complex social self, are yielding a remarkable mosaic, one that speaks with clarity and power to the interwoven and complex relationships between our culture and the land. Alex MacLean's photographs and James Corner's collage overlays and writings reveal some of the origins and processes of the patterns that are still evolving in the contemporary American-built landscape. Their remarkably vivid images provide clues for deciphering the sources and qualities of the constructed landscape.

The Corner-MacLean project—and the new landscapes it suggests—is reminiscent of Le Corbusier's speculation about the American grain elevator earlier in the century, chronicled in his *Toward a New Architecture*. Le Corbusier's encounters with these elevators and his observations on their form had great consequences for modern architecture, motivating architects to design buildings as reflections of the modern machine age. Corner's and MacLean's work may portend a similar period of design significance for landscape architecture. Like a divining rod bending toward the earth, this book points to enormous physical, environmental, and social changes that determine the form of the contemporary landscape, changes not unlike the upheavals that occurred during the pre–Le Corbusier era. Implicit in these pages is the notion that the designed landscape can become a representation of the more anonymous cultural and regional landscape. The Corner-MacLean project is a contemplation of the complex, opaque, and ultimately remarkable process of how "undesigned" or common American landscapes might become sources for future landscapes that are more intentionally created as artifice.

Our need for inventive landscape designs that address the realities and challenges of the late twentieth century makes it imperative that we understand the evolution of the contemporary landscape surrounding us, that we "take the measure" of our collective inheritance. The vision articulated by Corner and MacLean in this book—framed ingeniously around spatial, ethical, and poetic themes of measure—is enormously helpful in this regard and may spark future observation by others on the evolution of new built landscapes and their implicit or explicit connections to the larger cultural landscape.

MICHAEL VAN VALKENBURGH

Erosion Berms across Red Soils with Green Field.
Chapel Hill, North Carolina.

PREFACE

This book is the outcome of a collaborative effort between Alex MacLean, a pilot and aerial photographer, and myself, a landscape architect. Our travels across the American landscape began in 1990 and continued, depending upon weather, time, and resources, in periodic bursts during the three years that followed. Initially, we set out to find those images that best exemplified the various agricultural and technological landscapes of America and to understand how these different environments had been forged over time. Our journeys took us to most regions of the United States, although in a country of 3,618,770 square miles there are doubtless many other places worthy of inclusion that we simply did not have an opportunity to see.

In general terms, this book could be read as a visual and descriptive survey of the American landscape. Perhaps the combination of aerial photograph, map, and text might also provide the casual reader with alternative or unusual ways of seeing the land. A closer reading of this book, however, should reveal a series of arguments and viewpoints that make the whole both more and less than a novel survey: more because this book extends and takes liberties beyond comprehensive description; and less because there is a focus and selectivity to the work that almost certainly fails to consider many other dimensions of the landscapes depicted. This book is, therefore, perhaps best read as a provisional pro-

Flight Line across the United States. 14 x 20".

ject, a rhetorical and speculative work that is intended to provoke thought about the making of the American landscape, the culture that lives upon it, and the possibilities for its future design.

The book is divided into two parts—one verbal and theoretical, the other visual and descriptive. The first part contains four short essays concerning the tripartite relationship among measure, aerial vision, and the cultural occupancy of land. Although a number of other works have presented aerial pictures of America, this section is intended to investigate more critically how landscape representation (especially that of aerial vision) not only reflects a given reality but also conditions a way of seeing and acting in the world.[1] In other words, how a particular people view, value, and act upon the land is in large part structured through their codes, conventions, and schemata of representation—their cultural *images*.

The first chapter, "The Measures of America," is an important contribution by the British geographer Denis Cosgrove. In it he discusses the cartographic and settlement practices that have led to the formation of the modern American landscape and contrasts these with European and various historical senses of land, environment, and aerial vision. In chapter 2, "Aerial Representation and the Making of Landscape," I briefly discuss the relationship of the aerial view to the work of interpretation, representation, and the planning and design of land. In chapter 3, a short essay entitled "The American Landscape at Work," I describe how the American landscape is more a complex network of material *activity* than it is a static and contemplative phenomenon. Chapter 4, "Taking Measure: Irony and Contradiction in an Age of Precision," deals with the various uses and ambiguities of modern measures, with a focus on those aspects of measure that are central to both the historical and future shaping of the American landscape.

Part two of the book demonstrates these arguments through illustrated essays composed of Alex MacLean's aerial photographs and a series of map-drawings and captions that I prepared. We begin by presenting practical and utilitarian examples of measure (survey, allotment, spacing, precautionary steps, and rules), and we end with instances of measure that reflect the imaginative, symbolic, and intangible aspects of human existence. Our intention is not to polarize these two aspects—the instrumental and the poetic—but to point toward new reciprocities between them. In many ancient societies, this semantic range was inseparable, a unity that has dissolved only recently during the modern era (beginning with the scientific revolution of the seventeenth century). One of the aims of this book is to restore—or, at least, to suggest—various poetic and ethical dimensions of measure, especially with regard to the practical structuring of human relations across the land.

The chapter entitled "Measures of Land" charts the way America was surveyed and settled, focusing upon the procedures of the National Land Survey, initiated by Congress in 1785. "Measures of Control" records some of the most remarkable examples of human technological prowess in controlling and transforming natural forces, including the water-control projects of the Colorado River and the windmill-turbine fields of southern California. "Measures of Rule" demonstrates the necessity of demarcations, schedules, and methodical procedures for the organization of activities upon the land, using various agricultural operations and transportational networks as illustrations. "Measures of Fit" shows how dimensional "fitting" can literally embody ecological and ethical choices (as in measures that are

"good", "correct", or "appropriate"). Images in this section are drawn from contemporary farming practices as well as from Native American settlements in the Southwest. "Measures of Faith," the last category, records a number of measures that have been taken to sustain and promote human hope, usually through their enabling of that which escapes all measurement to appear.

We intend this book to be accessible to a large and diverse audience. At the same time, we hope that it will stimulate those who work directly with the land (especially landscape architects and planners) to go beyond narrow stylistic and ameliorative debates and to recognize the creative role of measure in structuring immense landscapes that are both functional and expressive of human hope.

This desire is further expressed in the thoughtful contributions of Michael Van Valkenburgh and Denis Cosgrove. For their insights and reflections on this work, we are extremely grateful. We also wish to thank others who have shared our vision and helped shape this book: John Dixon Hunt, chairman and professor of Landscape Architecture at the University of Pennsylvania, has been a helpful colleague in reviewing draft manuscripts; Judy Metro, at Yale University Press, and Karen Gangel have extended to us patience, enthusiasm, and great editorial acuity; Karolos Hanikian, Saul Jabbawy, and Chris Zlocki were an enormous help in assembling parts of this project. We owe a special debt of gratitude to Anne-Marie and Kate for their support during our long hours away from home.

We shall always remember the countless people we met as we traveled across the country. Their generosity of spirit and imagination were a constant source of pleasure and inspiration. Many of these anonymous and larger-than-life Americans will probably never know the extent of their impact on this book, but they might at least begin to recognize their own measure-taking capacity in working the land and enriching our collective lives upon it.

The work collected in these pages was made possible by the generous support of the National Endowment for the Arts; the Graham Foundation for Advanced Studies in the Fine Arts; the Graduate School of Design, Harvard University; the Graduate School of Fine Arts, University of Pennsylvania; the University of Pennsylvania Research Foundation; and Landslides, Inc.

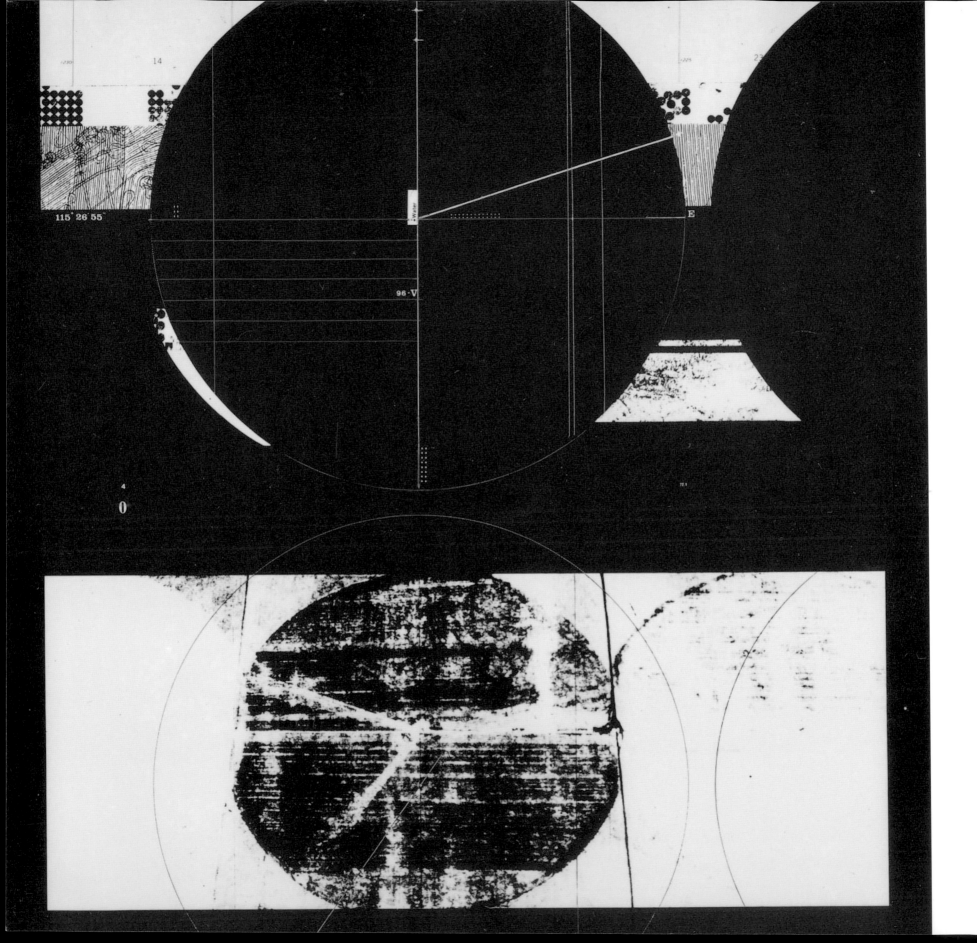

INTRODUCTION

Beginnings are perhaps most propitious if their ends are neither clearly envisaged nor defined. As with children at play, such indetermination can often precipitate unexpected findings, enabling one to discover new and unforeseen aspects in affairs that may seem ordinary or exhausted. At the start of our journeys across the American landscape, Alex MacLean and I hoped that such an open and flexible attitude would help us unearth new insights. Thus, our work together began in the spirit of free travelers, without any self-imposed restriction, agenda, or theoretical hypothesis. We were simply curious about the variety of landscapes that made up America. If there was an original motivation, it was simply our desire to experience and record some of the aerial vistas that are unique to the great landscapes of America; beyond this, our expectations were open-ended. We found, in fact, that this relaxed approach allowed us to cope with the overwhelming impossibility of traveling to every place in the United States and relieved us of the need to fully uncover the diverse temporal and cultural dimensions that inevitably surrounded the places we did visit.

Our initial method of negotiation with the land was to divide the country into geographical regions (for example, the Northwest, the Central Plains, the lower Mississippi), to travel to the center of each, and then to span outward as much as was prac-

Circular Irrigator Trace. 14 × 20″.

tically possible. We would sometimes take these trips together in MacLean's small Cessna. More often, however, I traveled by car or foot, while he flew alone, controlling the plane with his feet, as his head, hands, and camera hung out of the cockpit window.[1]

Although both of us relied heavily upon guidebooks, maps, and cameras, a series of chance encounters with people and land provided a greater sense of orientation. In fact, for all of the planning prior to a trip, we would still find ourselves wherever strange and unforeseen events led us.[2] The sudden effects of chance, error, and luck, dashing wildly across every rational scheme and purpose, were later to affect our appreciation of the various ways the American landscape had been forged, revealing the inevitable inadequacy of human determinations (measures) in the face of time.

Recordings

Initially, photography served as the primary means of recording our travels. Of course, in contrast to the motion of the traveler, the static nature of the photograph is unable to convey the temporal experiences of passage, the emerging and withdrawing of phenomena, and the strange ways events unfold. There is also a certain immediacy to the experience of a photograph, unlike the durational experience of narrative prose, movies, or soundtracks, for which sequential timing is essential. Nonetheless, the best photographs always entice and capture the imagination of the curious viewer, drawing him or her deep into the uniqueness of the moment. Created within a split second, pictures embody a finding that is unrepeatable; they hold an otherwise imperceptible time still for eternity. As Roland Barthes comments in *Camera Lucida,* this stillness and permanence is what makes a good photograph "uncanny";[3] it is transparent to its referent while also present as a photograph, sympathetic yet (in)different to its subject, like a ghost that is at once more and other than a simple lookalike. There is an odd autonomy to good photographs, wherein they acquire a status unto themselves and can no longer be considered mere representations. Instead, photographs, for all of their abstraction, have an oddly constitutive power in the shaping of reality and the perceiving of place and time.[4]

I had been aware of MacLean's aerial photographs for a number of years before our trips together, and I continue to be struck by their uncanny nature. In my work as a landscape architect, they have been both informative and inspiring. His pictures possess an internal eloquence and beauty while revealing aspects of the land that would otherwise remain hidden or unseen. Although MacLean's photographs are often strange and enigmatic, they are less abstract than they are matter-of-fact, extracting sections of the landscape and re-presenting them for scrutiny. MacLean's lens does not seek to obscure or distort; he rarely uses a filter and never does he manipulate the photograph in its printing. Instead, his pictures present the land *just as it is,* albeit under particular and rarely replicable viewpoints, circumstances, and moments of light. This momentary realism is complemented by the contemplative and slow manner in which a viewer must subsequently apprehend the photograph. Whereas the richness of color and graphic frontality often allow one to grasp the image immediately, the eye is still lured in and made to linger. It is very difficult to turn away from these pictures without a curious desire to return to them. The imagination roams across their topographical depths and the viewer is prompted to speculate about the narrative of the moment: What is it . . . Where . . . When . . . Who had been there, and what were they doing? This curiosity, evoked by the strangeness of the photograph, unsettles the immediacy of the first glance, and the image that was at first merely retinal then demands to be read more as a map or a visual text that must be decoded through imaginative interpretation. Here, the viewer becomes less a voyeur and more a participant in the piecing together of a visual puzzle or oddity. This engaging capacity of photographic representation, together with a desire to see and capture aerial America through the photographic medium, provided the initial impetus for our working together on this book.

As our travels proceeded we found ourselves increasingly drawn not only to the visual beauty of the land but also to the puzzle of its evolution and making. Moreover, because we believed the landscape to be as good a measure of cultural value and American ways of life as any other, we were in fact gauging the topographical facts of the land as reflections of the character of the society that had shaped it. Through a form of contemplative survey, we were attempting to take the measure of the American landscape, to take stock of a richly constructed inheritance.

The measures of the landscape were not, however, our only focus. While surveying the ground, we found ourselves continually caught up within the measures of our work—the methods, instruments, and practices that were inherent to our viewing. There were judgments, determinations, limits, and values that continuously underlay almost every choice of route, altitude, meeting place, schedule, map reading, lens, aperture, and timing; these would inevitably color our understanding of the landscape, prompting us to reflect upon the nature of representational method and its effect upon subsequent acts. Consequently, our attention finally settled upon the topic of measure, particularly the relationship between how measures employed in seeing the world affect actions taken within it and how particular kinds of reality are then constructed.

The photographs alone soon proved to be insufficient representations with regard to this new focus. Instead, the map, with its reference to scale and synoptic mode of presentation, increasingly assumed new levels of significance for us. Although we had always used maps to select and navigate routes, closer readings revealed features and measures that were not always explicit or visible upon the land itself. In turn, this kind of vision enabled a greater level of spatial and topographical understanding. I would often scribble over an old, crumpled map in an attempt to find structural relationships across the ground and to plot paths across it. These notations prompted me to make a series of map-drawings, which became composites of maps with photographic and satellite images, often overlaid with dimensional and logistical equations and other invisible lines of measure. The consistent use of the United States Geological Survey (U.S.G.S.) maps in the making of these drawings provides a seemingly neutral and objective field for the comparison and contrast of forms across regions; in addition, they provided precise orienting coordinates and other cartographic data crucial for navigation.[5] The inscriptions, additions, and deletions that were subsequently made to these maps embody an attempt to acknowledge the primacy of rational, synoptic measure in the forging of the American landscape while revealing the fictional and metaphorical dimensions of the land's construction.

As presented in this book, these map-notation drawings are meant to complement the photographs and at the same time to stand apart from them. Both types of image are aerial, offering a synoptic perspective, but the map-drawings play on certain planning abstractions, such as making visible strategic organizations of elements across a ground plane or revealing certain scale and interrelational structures (from regional to local networks of communication, for example). Consequently, the drawings (but also the photographs, in a different and less explicit way) reveal how typically prosaic and analytical methods of synoptic planning and land systematization harbor a more poetic, creative potential.

Measures

It is perhaps paradoxical that the initial rambling and sifting through an immense, open-ended landscape would lead us to something as precise and determinate as measure. But, as we hope to argue, the determinations that are enabled by measure are themselves slippery and fictional, often veiling (or even denying) the fact that life—in its innate richness, diversity, and freedom—is predicated upon certain degrees of error, chance, and indetermination. This point is implicit throughout this book and is most elaborated upon in chapter 4, but it might be useful to introduce the various ways we have come to use the term *measure* here.

We sometimes use it in specific ways (relating to dimension, gauge, or precautionary step, for example) and sometimes in its full semantic range, encompassing certain spatial, ethical, and poetic themes at once. Here, not only quantities (numbers, dimensions, allotments) and instruments (utilitarian and technical means) are spoken of, but so too are measures of morality and justice (as in determinations of what is "good" and "proper"), together with various representational, reconciliatory, and poetic capacities of measure (as in the rhythms and harmonies of music, art, and cosmography).

Measure as quantum refers to perhaps the most obvious usage of the term: its numerical, dimensional, and quantitative function. In this sense, measure is the unit as well as the vehicle by which a particular reality is given a mathematical structure. For ancient societies, the numerical and proportional measure of things revealed the harmonious order of the natural world and thereby provided evidence of a divine and unified cosmos. Music, art, and science were all structured around mathematical harmonies *(mathesis)*, each disclosing the coherency of the universe and embracing the full metaphorical range of measure described above.[6] Today, however, knowledge of numbers, dimensions, tolerances, and capacities has shifted from the traditional representational and symbolic emphasis to more autonomous and instrumental functions, with human technologies being used more to dominate and control the natural world than to reveal culturally significant forms of order. In other words, modern developments in mathematical and scientific appropriations of measure have enabled humankind to create a range of remarkable measures that continue to improve human life on earth (reflecting the still-pervasive Enlightenment dream of infinite social progress through rational calculation), while certain existential and imaginative bases of human dwelling are ignored or diminished in value.[7]

Modern calculative technologies and standards characterize a second aspect of measure: that of the instrumental or the means taken to secure a particular end. Instruments—whether musical, mathematical, or technological—cannot, however, be considered separately from dimension and number. Quantum and instrument are bound together; measure enables the making of the instrument, although it is the instrument that allows for measure to appear and become available. A musical scale is dependent upon an accurately tuned instrument, for example, just as the provision of measured amounts of power and water in southern California is dependent upon the dams and canal systems along the Colorado River. In this sense, measure, as both quantum and instrument, affects how actions are taken in the world.

These resultant actions become a problem, however, when the producer of instruments neglects to attend to the social and cultural ends of their work, emphasizing instead the instrument (or the means) as an end in itself. The excesses of instrumentality are characterized in the "detached" development of the nuclear bomb, for example, or in the procedural execution of the Holocaust. These technocratic activities, apparently devoid of human reflection, are mirrored in less ominous but equally empty ways by the emphatic value modern society places on increased efficiency and utility. If things are not profitable, useful, or of immediate and measurable benefit, they are often deemed to belong to the domain of the romantic and deluded. Philosophers and thinkers of the past two centuries have argued that this situation is symptomatic of a larger anthropocentric obsession with power and domination. Among the many deleterious consequences of this modern paradigm have been the reduction and homogenization of life and place-forms, as well as the many social and ecological ills that continue to plague human relationships with the earth.

Thus, the numerical and instrumental values that guide the use of measure point to a third meaning of the term, one contained in the distinction between what is "good," "just," or "correct" and what is "bad," "inappropriate," or "wrong." Through their dimensions, proportions, and instruments, measures inevitably convey various levels of ethical and social propriety. Consequently, the measures employed and enacted across the land—legislatively, spatially, technologically—are themselves measures of a society's ethos, expressed most poignantly in the interplay of appearance, usage, and cultural codes of representation. In this understanding, number and utility may be conjoined with beauty and virtue, a potential that many ancient societies recognized but that many in the modern world appear to have forgotten.

Illustrated throughout the book is this tripartite play on the meaning and agency of measure. The interrelationship of numerical, instrumental, and ethical dimensions of measures taken across the land, together with the potential for greater reciprocity and poetry between them, forms the basis of the following words and images. The American landscape is herein presented as a densely measured construction site made up of survey lines, clearings, highways, railroads, hedgerows, fields, canals, levees, dams, buildings, towns, and other spacings, constructs, and marks that secure settlement and enable human occupation of land. Consequently, the way a particular landscape looks is considered inseparable from, and integral to, the day-to-day activities and values of its occupants. In this way, quality and value cannot be detached from quantity, just as spacings, tolerances, and limits cannot be considered separately from ideology, ethics, and social responsibility. Thus, the measures of land have a threefold nature: they are at once the guide, the outcome, and the gauge of cultural activity and meaning.

One of our intentions in this book is to show how actions taken upon the land can either precipitate or preclude the possibility for more wholesome and harmonious modes of dwelling. We wish to argue that to continue to relate to the land either as an exploitable resource or as merely a scenic phenomenon is to fail to recognize the dynamic and interactive connectedness between human life and the natural environment. We do not wish to suggest a return to a pretechnological age or to promote romantic illusions of Arcadian life upon the land; instead we seek to restore to measure its full metaphoricity—its full capacity for representation—especially as this might forge new forms of interrelationship between people and land. Although we hope to disclose various imaginative extensions of measure and geometry, we do not deny the emancipating power of modern technology.

Perhaps our ultimate intention in this book is to show how the increased precision of modern calculative rationality—with its universal, linear, and methodical rigor—lies (ironically) at the very source of all that is successful and exhilarating in modern life, on the one hand, and of all that is failing and vulgar, on the other. From the detached and synoptical view of the bird, this modern paradox is graphically expressed in the constructions and traces that mark the ground. From above, the various relationships among physical dimensions, human activities, natural forces, and cultural values can be seen to be as orderly, productive, and sophisticated as they are brutal and errant.

Through the use of photographs, map-drawings, captions, and essays, we intend to reveal how the measures of the American landscape are of marvelous and paradoxical dimension. Perhaps, if our culture can recognize, build upon and, at the same time, resist the various capacities of modern measure taking, we may come to realize that freedom and democracy are in fact predicated upon restraint and limitation, just as factual precision is predicated upon fictional errancy. Such dialectical syntheses may be the only realizable way to avoid single-minded tyranny on the one hand and meaninglessness on the other; they may also be the bases upon which imaginative forms of measure taking might enrich the modern cultural world and precipitate new, creative possibilities for human dwelling on the earth—measures of beginnings that harbor indefinite ends.

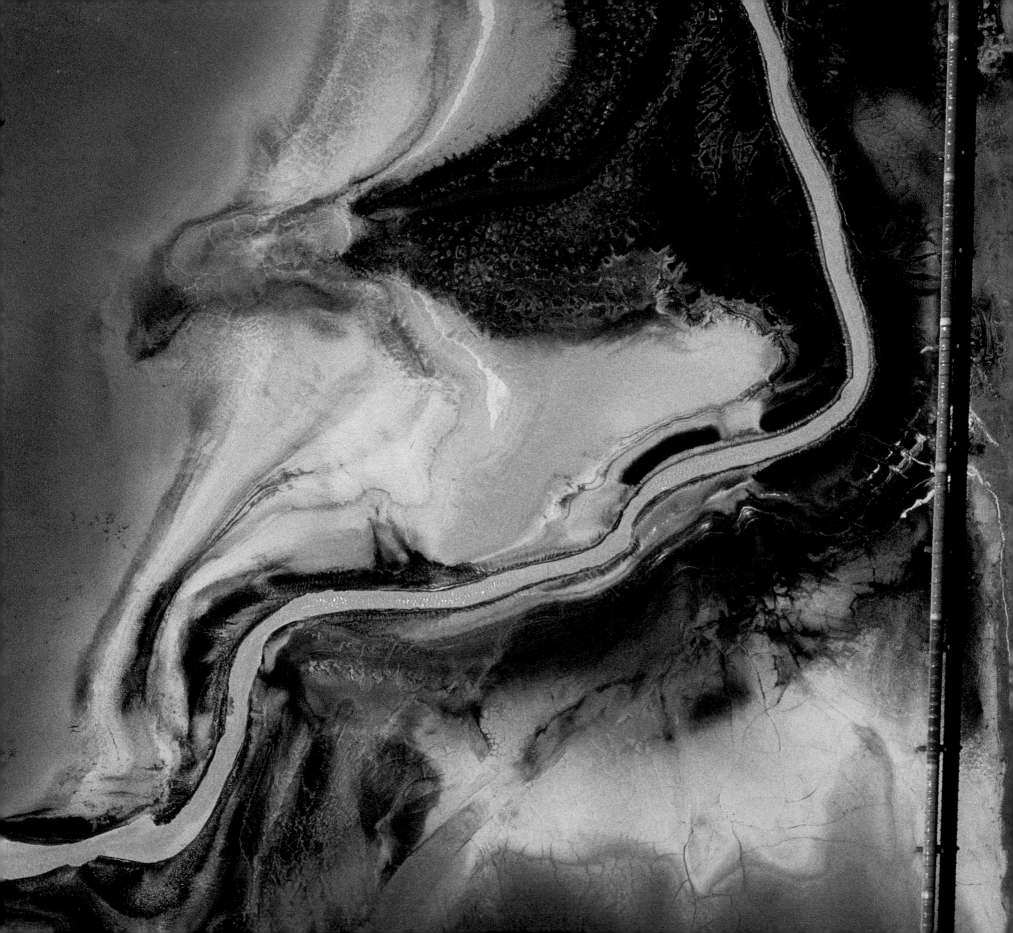

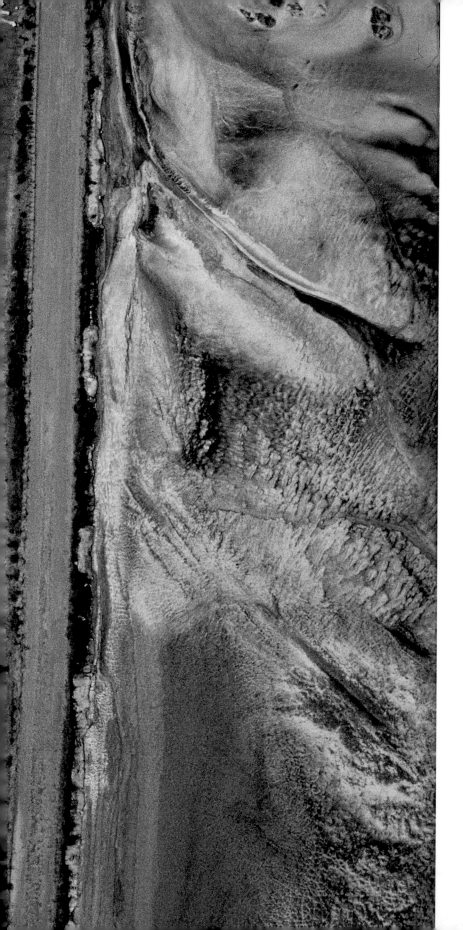

Part One

ESSAYS

Industrial Waste Settlement Pond. Savannah, Georgia.

CHAPTER I

THE MEASURES OF AMERICA

Denis Cosgrove

The American landscape makes sense from the air. This is not so true for elusive European landscapes, which level with the observer more slowly, only as we enter into them. European visitors to North America, from John Winthrop to Hector St. Jean de Crèvecœur to Jean Baudrillard, have all, in their different ways, recorded a common experience that becomes increasingly apparent as one travels west across America: that here *milieu* gives way to *space*. And Americans themselves—for example, the painter Albert Bierstadt—have been awed by the vastness of America's spaces and the scale of American nature. The term *sublime*, invented as a description of landscape in the eighteenth century, around the time of American independence, seems especially appropriate for the landscape of the United States. Walt Whitman and Frederick Jackson Turner went so far as to proclaim territorial space the very foundation of America nationhood. In popular culture, freight-train blues or the highway ballad still relay the romance of endless movement toward a specifically American horizon.

There are deep historical and cultural reasons for the distinction between American landscape and European landscapes and between the distanced, synoptic perspective by which American landscape is most clearly revealed and the intimate, fragmented view appropriate to European locales. Those reasons are closely connected to the ideas of measure that structure this collection of images. Because I am a European, Alex MacLean's aerial views and James Corner's responsive map-drawings stimulate me to reconsider the historical and cultural forces that have measured and structured American landscape. For the past half a millennium, those forces have been dominantly European in origin and American in outcome. The beliefs, desires, and visions inherent therein, originally nurtured in the crowded, fragmented, and bellicose little worlds of that splintered, subcontinental peninsula that is Europe, have been inscribed onto what, in European colonialist eyes, was essentially a vast, blank space. In the process of inscription, earlier cultural impressions on American nature—ancient mounds created by unknown peoples along the Mississippi in Illinois, or the Hopi village and Navajo pueblo in the arid Southwest—have been set adrift within the refashioned landscape, reduced to relict, archaeological echoes of past modes of human existence, which to contemporary eyes are largely of romantic appeal. They have become little more than ciphers of a cosmographic measure often believed to be absent in modern America.

Why is the aerial perspective so appropriate for imagining and understanding the American landscape? In selecting measure as their theme, Corner and MacLean have hit upon a significant part of the answer. According to the modern measure of time, we are living through the dying years of the twentieth century, at the closing of the second millennium. This has been the American century, and American culture has always been attracted to millenarianism; it structures much of the cultural landscape of the

Irrigated Fields in Desert. Holtville, California.

United States. This century opened with the insertion of Oklahoma as the final piece in the geometric jigsaw of coterminous states. It also opened with human conquest of the air, in North Carolina in 1903. Throughout the twentieth century a recurrent question has concerned the cultural and political implications of humanity's conquest of the air. In this essay, I shall highlight two seemingly contradictory, but closely related, responses to that question. Each concerns ways of measuring earth, expressions, we might say, of a geographical imagination. One concerns space, the other nature.

The airplane is the most visible of a great range of modern technologies that have progressively annihilated space by time over the course of this century.[1] The frictional effects of distance, the time and energy expended in moving across space, so painfully apparent on sea and land, are dramatically reduced in flight. The boundaries that fragment terrestrial space disappear in flight, so that space is reduced to a network of points, intersecting lines and altitudinal planes. Connections between disparate places become easy, even routine, with the consequence that place distinctions seem to fade, nowhere more apparently than in locations associated with flight: in airports, hotels, or leisure resorts.[2] The earth's topography flattens out to a canvas upon which the imagination can inscribe grandiose projects at an imperial scale. From the air, earlier impositions of political authority over space can be more fully appreciated: the die-straight linearity of Roman military roads, the geometry of Baroque urban plans, the gridded fields of reclaimed polderlands, the sweeping masonry curves of China's Great Wall. Since the 1920s, Modernist planners and architects have been captivated by the aerial view. The dream of flight, offering an Apollonian view of the wide earth, encouraged their visions of rational spatial order to be written across the land, without the hindrance of local contingency and variation. From this perspective, the political and cultural impacts of human flight revolve around the capacity for synoptic vision, rational control, planning,

and spatial order. A continental-scale nation such as the United States offered the practical as well as the imaginative canvas for such schemes.

Alternatively, and sometimes simultaneously, the aerial view has encouraged a new sensitivity to the bonds that exist between humanity and the natural world. Consider the introductory address of E. A. Gutkind, a planner and architect, at the 1956 conference entitled "Man's Role in Changing the Face of the Earth." Gutkind, who had been centrally involved in the physical reconstruction of Europe after both World Wars, claimed that "today we can look at the world with a God's-eye view, take in at a glance the infinite variety of environmental patterns spread over the earth, and appreciate their dynamic relationships."[3] Gutkind believed that such a view encourages synthetic rather than analytic thought: "Everything falls into a true perspective—even man himself as an integral part of the whole." With the help of nearly fifty aerial photographs, Gutkind drove home the central theme of the symposium—that humans are at once insignificant against the great measure of nature yet capable (if man's is the only measure) of wreaking the virtual destruction of earth as a home for human—and possibly all—life. What Gutkind recognizes is that the measure of nature is situated and contingent and thus that the aerial view can lead to a renewed appreciation of the organic and the local.

The ability to see the world from above culminated in the *Apollo* photograph of the spherical earth, whole and unshadowed, taken in 1972. Responses to that image have stressed the unity of the global vision coupled with the need for local sensitivity in a globalized world.[4] Commentators have echoed Gutkind in stressing that such a graphic demonstration of unity between humanity and nature should have lasting and positive effects on our social and environmental thinking.

Nowhere have these two themes—of space annihilated by time and of an ecological unity of nature and human life threatened by our own hubris—played themselves out more vocally than in the United States, in part because of the pivotal economic, political, and cultural role the country has played in the twentieth century. But, arguably, that role has simply allowed long-standing American predilections about land and life to become global ones. To understand those attitudes, one needs to recognize the historical character of Americans' social relations with space and nature and therefore to "take the measure" of the American landscape.

During the late fifteenth and early sixteenth centuries, America was blank space for the Genoese, Spanish, and Portuguese navigators who sailed from the Mediterranean into the open Atlantic. Indeed, even this truism is exaggerated in light of subsequent knowledge, for North America became a continent in the European consciousness only very slowly—and perhaps not fully until Lewis and Clark reached the Pacific coast early in the nineteenth century. For its initial discoverers, America was another group of islands in the Ocean Sea—like Madeira, the Canaries, or the Azores. Yet these same Europeans knew the dimensions of the globe, theoretically from Eratosthenes and experientially from Ferdinand Magellan's circumnavigation of 1522. America may have been blank space, but it was measured space. It was locally fixed by a grid of astronomically determined lines: latitude and longitude.

That graticule of latitude and longitude represents an abstract, intellectual inscription of measure across the globe. It is a measure determined by astronomical movements, the expression of spherical geometry. The Greeks believed that geometry had originated in Egypt with the practical need to redraw property lines after the annual Nile flood erased all terrestrial markers from the fields. But if directed toward practical ends on earth, geometry had its origin in the heavens, and it presupposed a distanced, rational perspective on space. Thus, the ancients also acknowledged the Platonic aspects of geometry, as a pure product of mind with immutable and therefore divine properties. It is impossible to separate the history and uses of geometry from those of cosmography and cosmology, the practicalities of latitude and longitude from the poetics of mathematical measure.

Children of the revival of classical knowledge during the Renaissance, European discoverers of the New World were fired by similar belief in the powers of geometry. The cultural world that launched the Columbian encounter possessed a profound belief in the power of mathematical measure.[5] It had created new spaces of representation in its art by applying perspective geometry to painting; it had revived the geometric measures of ancient Greek and Roman architecture; and it had rediscovered Ptolemy's astronomical techniques of map making. Geometry was the Renaissance measure of Man, that cultural invention of the years of discovery, whom the Renaissance philosopher Giovanni Pico della Mirandola placed midpoint between heaven and earth, angel and animal, and whom Leonardo located perfectly within circle and square.[6] Geometry united humanity and nature; it was the secret measure by which God's original creation had been ordered and sustained. It thus behooved God's highest creatures to employ that same measure in making their own, lesser worlds. Through geometric measure, Man would author the earth and, most especially, a new-found land to the West. Pope Alexander VI's longitudinal line of 1493, separating Spanish space from Portuguese in America, was thus the first act in a continuous intellectual measuring and shaping of the New World by European geometry. Slowly, the outlines of a continent would be inscribed within the great checkerboard frame of the graticule, while the checkerboard itself was transferred onto America's spaces in the form of property lines—of colonies, states, communities, and individuals.

In the European making of American space, therefore, cartographic measure predates and prefigures the meeting with nature. Colonists believed that the Native American population (referred to as savages, from *selvatici*, meaning "of the woods") was so much a part of nature that such creatures were incapable of the disembodied, aerial view implied by geometric measure. Captain

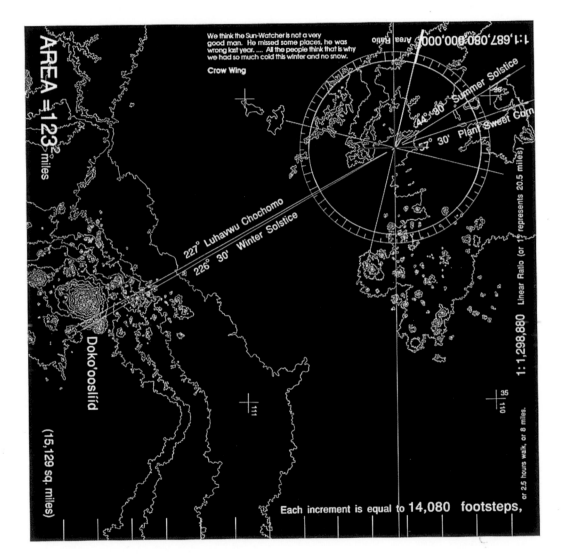

John Smith claimed of the natives of Virginia: "They are as ignorant of Geography as of other Sciences, and yet they draw the most exact Maps imaginable of the Countries they're acquainted with, for there's nothing wanting in them but the Longitude and Latitude of Places."[7]

We know how mistaken these Europeans were.[8] The contrary evidence is most apparent in the ancient landscapes of the Southwest. Locations at Hopiland, or the circles and squares at Pueblo Bonito, were founded on the same precise astronomical measurement and resonate with the same mathematical poetics as those of ancient Attic temples or the courtyards at Renaissance Urbino. By placing these measures against a background of the gridded United States Geological Survey (U.S.G.S.) map, James Corner drives home this point. The measure of the skies has a cosmic finality whose relations with terrestrial nature demand a constant intellectual attention. If their measure is somehow wrong, nature itself is affected: "the time is out of joint."

As recognition of the scale of a new world gradually dawned on colonists and Europeans, they searched for some mode of coming to terms with and controlling the immensity of American space as well as the difference of American nature. Measuring and mapping, imagining the landscape in the mind, or inscribing it onto paper are more rapid, less dangerous, and more secure ways of coping with unknown spaces than penetrating the Appalachian forests with axe or trekking the featureless grasslands of the Llano Estacado. The map offers a way of controlling both the contingencies of nature and the rivalries of human proprietors. In the settlement of America, each community faced the joint need to balance the freedoms and physical dangers offered by immeasured space against the safety and social constraint offered by measure, rule, and boundary.

Hopi Horizon Calendar. 14 × 20".

Transferring the map from parchment or paper to the ground itself creates American landscape out of American nature and European imaginings. This process too has its own history, a history inflected by the cultural backgrounds of settlers and the environmental context in which they found themselves. In the dense forests of the eastern seaboard and the lake and river areas of the Northeast, measure by the stars was rarely possible in any consistent manner. Little wonder then that the French—*coureurs du bois,* whose search for furs in the forests of North America took them from their snowbound St. Lawrence landfall through the Great Lakes and the Ohio, Mississippi, and Missouri systems—used the lines of the riverbanks as the baseline for their cartographic surveys and property systems. Straight property lines, or *rangs,* leading back from the banks of a meandering river inevitably diverge or converge and produce fanlike patterns whose logic is apparent from the map or the air. At first sight, such a cadaster may seem more responsive to the contingencies of nature than the astronomically determined patterns of the Anasazi pueblo in the treeless Southwest or the Anglo-Saxon grid across the prairies. But rivers, especially those that flow in the vast floodplains of the Mississippi valley, alter their courses with a regularity that leaves the long-lot landscapes of Louisiana frequently disconnected from the water frontage that determined their initial logic.

The scale of these rivers, like the scale of much of American nature, was quite out of proportion to anything that European settlers had ever experienced. One of the few words left to us by the obliterated native peoples of the Caribbean is *hurricane,* a natural phenomenon of such violence as to be unnameable in any European language.[9] Despite the endeavors of European thinkers (such as Count Georges-Louis Buffon) to represent American nature as degenerate (based on the paucity of large mammals), with the intention of elevating Europe to the peak of an imagined evolutionary hierarchy, those who actually confronted American nature more frequently experienced its enormous scale and power:

the endlessness of its forests, the height and power of its water-falls, the dimensions and fury of its storms, the numberless herds of buffalo and flocks of passenger pigeons that covered the plains and blotted out the sun. The sublimity of American nature is exemplified in the records of the Lewis and Clark expedition, sent out by Thomas Jefferson to describe the landscapes of the newly acquired West and to disprove such slights as Buffon's to American nature, especially as the explorers moved beyond the Great Falls of the Missouri into the mountainous West.[10]

Jefferson's role in the making of American space is central. Historically, movement of European settlement beyond the eastern forests onto the open prairie grasslands coincided with the young republic's great democratic experiment to ensure for its people "liberty, a farmyard wide."[11] For the Founding Fathers, children of the European Enlightenment, and above all for Jefferson, mathematical measure was not so much the divine attribute it had been to America's Renaissance discoverers as the tool through which the moral and social goals of a new nation could be achieved. Rational monetary measure (dollars and cents rather than pounds, shilling, and pence); rational weights and measures (the reformed gallon and the geographic mile); and rational division of land into rectangular states, townships, and sections—all these were intended to create a new and more perfect society. And it was the "open" American space to the West that offered the great historic opportunity to achieve this ancient European dream of utopia, space for which Jefferson devised a method of individual property division and which, as president, he set about purchasing, exploring, and mapping.

The rectangular survey system, whose square townships, die-straight property lines and field boundaries, and abrupt discontinuities dominate the agrarian landscape of the United States west of the Appalachians, may seem, through our ecologically sensitive eyes, an expression of human insensitivity to nature. But we should recall its original intention within the context of a

European culture, in which citizenship had always been founded upon ownership of immobile property, that is, upon land. Opening American space in equally sized parcels, at an affordable price, to individual farmers appeared the precondition for a stable and open democracy. The rectangular grid is the perfect spatial expression of the republic's democratic imperative. Although the axially converging lines of the princely Renaissance city or the Baroque garden speak of aristocratic power and centralized authority, the grid privileges no one point above another. It is the landscape measure of America's commitment to life, liberty, and the pursuit of happiness, distributing power equally across space. And the vastness of this conception, corresponding in its universality to the Enlightenment belief in a single, rational order in nature, is a fundamental determinant of America as *landscape* rather than as *landscapes*.

The foundational principle of land allocation (enunciated by the Land Ordinance Act of 1785, which established the rectangular survey) was that land should be surveyed and recorded on the plat before settlement. Although this principle, like the strictures against speculation, may have been honored as often in its breach as in its application, it reinforced the cartographic foundation of American social space, laying the surveyor's measure across nature's local contingencies. The insistency of its geometric logic is most apparent on the U.S.G.S. topographic map, on which the design conventions and choice of landscape elements to be represented privilege geometry over topography. The American topographic sheet is a network of intersecting lines and numbered squares; no European map is so fiercely linear and numerical. It is appropriate that Corner's drawings consistently use the topographic sheet as the base for taking measures across the American landscape. On the ground, matters are different. The grid confronts us in the straight road with its sudden dogleg turn to accommodate an adjustment, in the regularity of passing farmsteads in Illinois or Ohio landscapes, but in little else. Only from the air does the global insistence of its controlling geometry reflect that of the map (pls. 8, 9).

For nature, too, has its insistences. Even across the horizontal field squares of the Great Plains, the dendritic geometry of water courses strikes across the rectangularity of survey lines. Elsewhere it may be the relict features of the geologic past that interrupt the universality of Enlightenment landscape logic with an entirely different temporal measure: drumlin fields, kettle holes, and eskers in the Northern Plains that speak of ice advances and retreats, measured according to a geological time scale (pls. 10, 11). What is remarkable in their appearance from the air is that it is these features of nature that seem out of place in a paper landscape rather than the human measure seeming inappropriate in the context of such huge and ancient natural forces. On the ground, the relative roles are reversed, as the human landscape appears to submit to natures's prior and unchallengeable claims.

On the map such natural features appear as contour lines—islands in a charted sea whose curving, intricate patterns seem almost to subvert the logic of rectangular geometry imposed by the grid. As European settlement moved beyond the humid lands of the Missouri-Mississippi plains, out into the semiarid and arid West, the tensions between nature's measures and those imposed by human minds became even sharper. The West was won, we know, not by the frontier people or the pioneer wagon train but by the railroads. Before the townships and ranges of the federal land surveyors could be turned into a checkerboard of fields and crops, the railroad engineers and navigators had to bolt lines of steel across the continent. More than any other technologies, the railroad, and its inseparable partner, the electric telegraph, were responsible for the annihilation of space by time in the nineteenth century. As everywhere, it was the timetable demands of the rail corporations that first required a single measure of time to be imposed across the local measures that had previously prevailed.[12] America had to be remeasured in time

zones across its continental space. The locomotive turning circle that MacLean photographed in Minneapolis appears, appropriately, almost like a great clock face in the landscape, controlling the times and distances across the network—an image captured in Corner's rail-network drawing (pls. 58, 59). That network often cuts uncompromisingly the rectangular property grid, and the towns and regularly spaced grain elevators aligned to its tracks record the supremacy of corporate railroad-barons' interests over the Jeffersonian vision of the independent yeoman in the western landscape (pls. 12, 13).

Confidence that nature had been nailed down by geometry was shared by both railroad boosters in New York and Chicago and isolated homesteaders on their quarter or half-quarter sections that stretched across Oklahoma and the Texas Panhandle with only the rail line to measure an endless horizon. Such confidence was misplaced. Only the most sensitive adjustment to the vagaries of local nature will allow continued cultivation west of the hundredth meridian.[13] Contour plowing and other dry-farming techniques have been the precondition of Plains agriculture since the environmental and the social catastrophe of the Dust Bowl.[14] Thus even in the most topographically featureless regions of the United States, where the linearity of survey line and railroad track seem the supreme and unchallenged measure of the landscape, nature indirectly reasserts a different measure. It is the serpentine line of the contour, once again revealed by survey and cartographic convention: the measure of level. The contour lines of natural topography, scarcely apparent on the ground, are highlighted from the air or on soil conservators' maps in the bands and colors of alternating cropland, weaving a more complex landscape texture across the warp of the rectangular survey (pl. 86).

This landscape of contour plow lines dates from the mid-twentieth century, from the years of the New Deal, when, for the first time since Jefferson's mastering vision for the continental landscape, the federal government became involved in large-scale landscape planning. As in the Land Ordinance, the landscape was envisioned first through survey and map: in this case, of less visible elements, such as soil quality and aquifers, rather than of simple topography. But now the planners had another technology at their disposal: the airplane and the aerial photograph. With it came the combination of synoptic vision and local sensitivity we encountered above. A buzzword of Modernist engineering, whether in aircraft design or in hydrological planning, was *streamline*. The streamline implied more than just speed—the latest stage in the conquest of space by time; it also implied rational, scientific efficiency through adjustment to natural flows.[15] Water and air always follow the path of least resistance around obstacles. Such flows suggest a paradigm for human interventions in nature, allowing natural properties to be directed toward human ends, as in the case of flight itself, where air flows over the plane's wing and lifts the craft off the ground.

Some Modernist planners and architects recognized the affinities between the idea of the streamline and the Chinese cosmological concept of *feng-shui* (literally, wind-water), which acts within Chinese cultural tradition as an elemental measure of human interventions in the natural landscape. Attention to feng-shui ensures that the spirit of place is not offended by injudicious intervention. The streamline makes such adjustment visible in landscape form, revealing it in the flowing motion of the contour furrow and the curving meander of the regulated river (pl. 30).

Nowhere is the Modernist vision of streamlined planning more beautifully apparent in the American landscape than in those concrete monuments to Modernist visionary engineering, the great river dams and reservoirs of mid-century. Perhaps the finest monument to integrated planning and the synoptic vision of the American century is in the landscapes of dams and regulated curving river channels that make up the Tennessee Valley project. Today a strong ecological lobby is critical of the United States Corps of Engineers because it believes the Corps' interventions are founded on an arrogant disregard of nature and an assumption of technological supremacy. Whether or not this is true, the matured landscapes of the Tennessee Valley Authority (TVA) reveal an engineered sensitivity to natural lines that undermines such criticism. The only way the scope and intention of the TVA can truly be appreciated is to view the landscape from the air or on a map. It is measured in the shapes of the lakes formed behind the river dams and follows the natural lines of the land, tracing its contours up the valleys and counterpointing the serpentine forms and natural colors of terrain and water with the strong geometric lines and concrete tones of the dams.

This Modernist landscape of water regulation reaches its apotheosis in the West, where the dams and power barrages on the Columbia, the Colorado, and the Snake river systems are true monuments to the concrete sublime. Such a claim is, I realize, somewhat unfashionable, and I am not denying that many of the long-term ecological consequences of such radical and large-scale interventions have been seriously detrimental. But it is important to recognize that within the limits of technological understandings of nature, such visionary engineering was intended to harmonize with the natural landscape, to respond to the elemental scale of the western rivers and their environs. Works along the Columbia and Snake Rivers, for example, were thought to enhance western nature and to maximize the potential of the area through means of irrigation and electrification, thereby creating a garden of the Pacific Northwest, a utopian landscape as genuine as Thomas Jefferson's. And the Grand Coulee Dam is indeed appropriate in scale and majesty to the Cascade Mountains, the Columbia Gorge, the forests and deserts that surrounded it.

In the truly arid intermontane West, the vast continental interior that occupies one-fourth of the breadth of the American continent, garden landscape gives way to wilderness. Islands of human occupancy, their location authorized by the presence of water, are all that have ever been possible for settlers in an elemental environment where burning sunlight, stinging wind, and hard-bitten rock otherwise repel human dwelling. Historically, Native Americans found oases in the cool depths of the canyon walls or replicated their protective shadows in the geometry of adobes set into the mesa (pls. 89, 90). Mormon farmers were among the first to introduce the Europeans' rectilinear geometry into their irrigated plots along the valley washes of Utah. And today center-pivot irrigation arms inscribe their precise circles into the rectangular fields of the land survey, producing vast mandalas across the western landscape (pls. 43–48). Water, the key element of life, exists far below the surface in deep aquifers, made visible in the landscape by technology. Here, among the most uncompromising nature that America can offer, the Renaissance measure of man is visible from the air or on the map as a circle of green alfalfa set into a square of brown desert.

MacLean and Corner respond knowingly to the elemental aspects of this western landscape. Wind and fire, as well as water and earth, dominate their photographs and designed images. Controlled burning is a significant technique in the management of grain fields, returning nutrients to the soil while clearing pests in the stubble (pls. 61, 62). In the great western forest lands, in large measure now given over to national parks and forests, fire has always been a powerful element of renewal, and the appropriate extent to which humans should intervene to control fire as a landscape element in regions artificially protected from natural development has been a matter of fierce debate over the past decade. Corner's image of a burned map, apparently by the use of a magnifying glass, recalls the power of the solar fire as a direct force in shaping and renewing the western landscape itself.

The closest that human technology has come to replicating the energy of the sun is in nuclear fission. Nuclear power has an elemental quality appropriate to the nature and scale of the western landscape, yet through nuclear development and testing, large areas of the intermontane West have been devastated: littered with the detritus of abandoned military hardware or rendered unfit for habitation in the foreseeable future by unexploded ordnance or radiation. The landscapes of the nuclear sublime are not represented here, although they have been captured photographically by Richard Misrach.[16] But the military presence in the West is more pervasive than simply its nuclear representation: huge air bases, missile-testing grounds, and bombing ranges—such as White Sands and Fort Bliss, in New Mexico; Nellis, in Nevada; Wendover, Deseret, and Dugway, in Utah—cover areas the size of some of the smaller European states.

The military landscape is not always malign. At Magdalena, which stretches under the cloudless skies of New Mexico, the three 15-mile tracks of the Very Large Array Radio Telescope, each with their nine receiving dishes, record the messages of planetary bodies, capturing celestial power and concentrating rays of energy in an attempt to make sense of the universe (pls. 114–19). Such activity is a fundamental feature of all cosmologies, archaic and contemporary. Hopi and Navajo solar observations are recorded in the locations and forms of their settlements. The cosmographic measure is not lost to the American landscape. We continue to use the same geometries of circles and intersecting lines as they to take the measure of the cosmos.

From the perspective of Europe, California and the West Coast is where the American landscape must end. "Beyond" is no longer West but the Far East. The utopian strain that has counted for so much in the social measure of the American experiment is most intense here. Gold attracted Europeans to California; climate kept them. California was not the only New World landscape to be promoted as America's Mediterranean. Georgia and Texas both enjoyed the same title in earlier times. But California more than either of those regions promised to fulfill the dreams of an Arcadian landscape in which a mythic memory of the glories of ancient Greece and Rome or of Renaissance Italy could somehow be revived.[17] Traces of that dream abound in contemporary

California landscapes: in its housing styles, the suburban landscaping of the great cities, or the vineyards of the Napa Valley. It is fascinating to discover unconscious echoes of the European Mediterranean within a truly American cultural landscape. The illustrated part of this book captures two such echoes. In Oceanside (pl. 64), fields of flower beds regulate one of the most potent symbols of the Mediterranean: the cultivated flower garden, within the rigid geometry of the American grid, producing slices of color, almost like slides of a spectrum.

More dramatic still are the windmills outside Los Angeles, set against mountains whose dry forms resemble those of Attica or the Peloponnese (pls. 37–42). Situated on the edge of a city that represents the apotheosis of American culture, the fluted columns rise like the structural elements of ancient Doric temples, which were built at sacred places where the spirit of the gods they honored were manifest. These structures responded to the genius loci as sensitively as a Chinese temple responds to feng-shui, and they were carefully oriented to forms on the horizon and patterns of sky and sea. Modern windmills are equally, if less mythologically, sensitive to both topography and wind. In the California landscape they convey a sense not only of the Mediterranean dream to use the New World to rediscover and reform Europe's golden age but of America's true cultural achievement: to draw upon the insights of diverse peoples from across the Old World and rework them in a physical landscape that imposes its own measure over all human endeavors.

Measures of time and measures of space, measures of humanity and measures of nature. Taking the measure of America is an impossible task, at once cosmic and personal. From the air, a kind

Detail, plate 40.

of order becomes apparent, above all the insistent autonomy of the land, with its capacity to absorb and rework any human imposition, giving it meanings much richer than those intended by humankind. For humanity, the air is the midpoint between earth and stars; it is the most suitable place. We are not tied irrevocably to earth and water but are able to escape to the stars, even if temporarily, in our imagination. Nonetheless, we are unable to subsist in air and fire and are pulled back insistently to the body of the land.

In the same decade that America was discovered, Pico della Mirandola perfectly articulated this intermediate position when he described Adam as a creature of "indeterminate nature" whom God had placed in the middle of his cosmos, stating:

> *Neither a fixed abode nor a form that is thine alone nor any function peculiar to thyself have We given thee, Adam, to the end that, according to thy longing and according to thy judgement thou mayest have what abode, what form, and what functions thou thyself shall desire. The nature of all other beings is limited and constrained within the bounds of law prescribed by Us. Thou, constrained by no limits, in accordance with thine own free will, in whose hand We have placed thee, shall ordain for thyself the limits of thy nature.*[18]

In the succeeding five hundred years the American landscape has been fundamentally altered, transformed by economic, cultural, and technological forces whose origins were only dimly discernible in Pico's world. We are aware, in ways that Pico was not, of the limitations on human will imposed by those bonds that unite all nature. Yet his words ring true today as we look down on the American landscape, so powerfully crafted by the social and individual dreams of generations who have followed Pico. We can never fully escape our attachments—and our responsibilities—to the landscape, but neither should we stop dreaming.

U.S. COAST & GEODETIC SURVEY
BENCH MARK
FOR INFORMATION WRITE TO THE DIRECTOR, WASHINGTON, D.C.
$250 FINE OR IMPRISONMENT FOR DISTURBING THIS MARK.
1002
1967

AERIAL REPRESENTATION AND THE MAKING OF LANDSCAPE

In a small book entitled *Aircraft*, published in 1935, the Modernist architect Le Corbusier reflects upon new insights of the earth and human settlement as afforded by the view from the air. In describing how this new synoptic vision suggests an alternative attitude toward the planning and design of cities and regions, he writes: "It is as an architect and town-planner—and therefore as a man essentially occupied with the welfare of his species—that I let myself be carried off on the wings of an airplane, make use of the birds-eye-view, of the view from the air." Aloft, "the eye now sees in substance what the mind could only subjectively conceive; [the view from the air] is a new function added to our senses; it is a new standard of measurement; it is the basis of a new sensation. Man will make use of it to conceive new aims. Cities will arise out of their ashes."[1]

Expressed in this remark is a fascination with both the experience of flight and the aerial machine itself. Certainly, this new sensation can be exhilarating for even the most seasoned pilot, especially in a small plane, from which landscapes unfold with kaleidoscopic grandeur. When one flies close to the ground, horizons, topographies, colors, textures, and gravities shift and turn in unexpected and breathtaking ways. During less acrobatic flights, the bird's-eye view prompts one to reflect upon the remarkable capacity of humankind to colonize and transform the surface of the earth. From high above, the American landscape appears as a patchwork of geometric regulation, punctuated by odd circles and large clusters of settlements. The ground is crossed by meandering rivers and diverging, straight lines of highways, railroads, canals, and transmission cables. Nearly all four million square miles of the United States have been marked in some way by people. Here, some of humankind's most extensive measures (many as destructive as others are productive) are revealed with detached and analytical clarity. More than the mere aesthetic of flight, this ability to see and conceive large regions from the air, with rational and comprehensive understanding, is what first inspired Le Corbusier and other Modernist planners. Subsequently, throughout the twentieth century, the aerial representation of land might be less significant for its scenographic perspective than for its instrumental utility in the modernization of the earth's surface. In other words, the aerial view has not only captured the imaginations of people around the planet but has also emerged as a powerful tool in the planning and shaping of regions.

What is revealed in this extensive visual panorama is an organic interdependency between humans and the natural world. Connecting vast physiographic regions, the interrelational ecology of the earth is perhaps best understood and manipulated from above. With synoptic rationality, the aerial view continues to inform and promote systematic planning of land across large, regional scales. Such planning methodology is described in Ian

United States Geological Survey Benchmark. Approximately 4" diameter in 18" square concrete. Taft Oil-field, California. (Photo by James Corner)

McHarg's seminal book *Design with Nature*, published in 1969, just after the first moon landing.[2] McHarg, widely credited as the pioneer of ecological landscape planning, opens his treatise with an *Apollo* photograph of the planet Earth, eerily alone in a great, empty universe. He supports his arguments and methods with additional satellite and remote-sensing views, aerial photographs, bird's-eye perspectives, and analytical maps and plans. Lavishly illustrated is an immense global project, conceived synoptically from above and promoting a rational planning of the land, if not actually aspiring to inventory and guide development across the entire planet. Whereas McHarg, like other environmentalists, occasionally portrays humankind as an enormous "planetary disease" (an image of scarring the earth's surface at a scale that would be unbelievable were it not for evidence provided by the aerial view), it is, ironically, the same humankind and its technology (aerial and otherwise) that he and other planners cite as the heroic arbiter and measure of all things. Paradoxically, the view from above induces both humility and a sense of omnipotent power.

Founded upon rational and technological instrumentality, the optimistic belief in social and economic progress has characterized American settlement and cultural life since the eighteenth century. The United States is predicated upon capitalist and entrepreneurial practices, wherein hard work and ingenuity will typically lead to profit and gain. The aerial view, with its analytical scope, is both a logical consequence and agent in this utopian scheme, a relationship that is especially reflected in the Land Division Survey of the late 1700s. Although the aerial photograph was obviously not available to the early surveyors of the United States, an aerial sensibility—expressed in Baroque, bird's-eye panoramic drawings, maps, and plans—nonetheless pervaded the rational construing, surveying, and colonizing of lands west of the Alleghenies. The endless rectilinearity of the United States survey was imposed maplike, as if from above,

with little or no regard for local variations in topography and ecology. The same attitude toward controlling the land from above continues today, for example, in the massive engineering projects that dominate entire river systems and span many physiographic regions or in the large-scale planning of transportation and communication infrastructure.

Many of these modern works would have been unimaginable—or at least unrealizable—without both the factual and imaginative dimensions provided by the first aerial representations of this century. Currently, advances in satellite imaging—with its capacity to record changes in the chemical composition of the biosphere, to represent global weather situations, and to correlate data with computerized geographic information systems—reflect just how sophisticated this synoptical view has become. It is a view that affects not only the cultural imagination but also the actions that human societies take, especially with regard to new policies and practices aimed toward regional and global ecology. As a consequence, these new technologies lead some in society to believe that humankind has supreme power and control over the earth, thereby encouraging plans for future economic and population growth; others (the majority of people) complain of a sense of individual helplessness, as if the fate of life is bound inaccessibly into large, highly specialized bureaucracies, institutions, and corporations.

The point here is not to induce apocalyptic grandeur but, rather, to suggest how the aerial view continues to affect modern cultural life and activities upon the land. The power of the aerial image lies less in its descriptive capacity—compelling as that is—than in its *conditioning* of how one sees and acts within the built environment. Like other instruments and methods of representation, the aerial view reflects *and* constructs the world; it

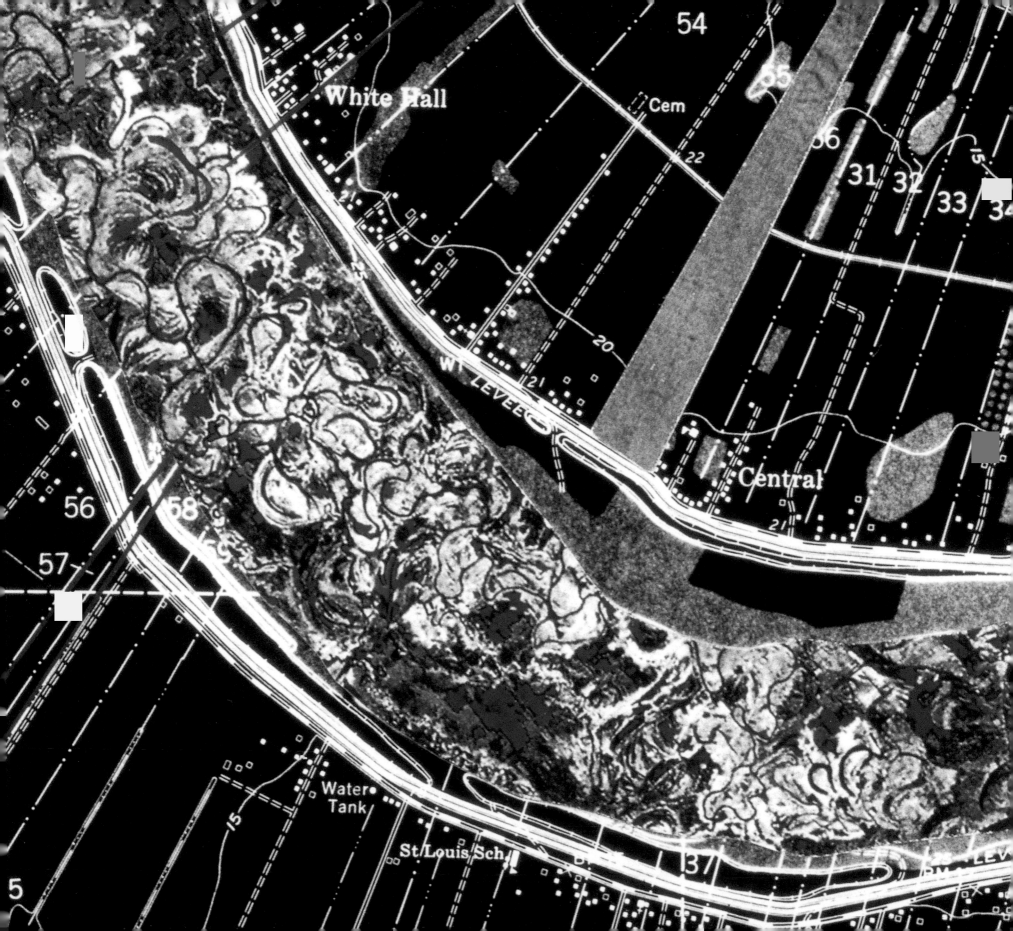

has enormous landscape agency, in real and imaginary ways. This point is evidenced in the fact that different people at different times see the same world in radically different ways; it is not the world that changes but the ways and means of seeing and acting. Description and projection entail taking a particular point of view—both spatial and rhetorical—that not only reflects a given reality but is also productive of one. Furthermore, as scholars and critics have recognized, the inescapable assumption of a viewpoint in representation is never neutral or without agency and effect; representation provides neither a mirror reflection of things nor a simple and objective inventory.[3] Instead, representations are projections, renderings of reality that are drawn from and thrown onto the world. Moreover, the history of painting, literature, and cartography has shown us that a mirror copy of the world—or a description that is so precise and truthful as to be an identical to the object it describes—is simply an impossible illusion and that the ontological presence of the representation itself is unavoidable.[4]

Consider the role of maps, for example, which, like aerial photographs or paintings, are documents that are not remotely like the land itself; they are flat, unidimensional, and densely coded with all sorts of signs and hieroglyphs. To read a map, one must be trained in cartographic conventions. But maps are not exactly incongruous with the land either, for they accurately reflect certain (selected) characteristics of it. Moreover, maps would have little meaning and utility without the prior condition of the land itself. Similarly, spatial and topographic awareness of a landscape would likely be limited and ambiguous without the prior knowledge of a map. Maps make visible what is otherwise invisible.

A number of geographers and cultural historians have described how maps are necessarily selective in content and can never exhaust the full range of interpretative meanings inherent to the experience of land, even though maps often lead readers to believe that they are looking at complete, objective descriptions of the land.[5] The fictional and incomplete characteristics of maps are often masked by the appearance of measured objectivity, as too are the effects that maps have upon people's future actions. Moreover, not only are these fictions the result of particular methods of construction (and, thus, only one outcome of many possible schemata), but they are also biased with regard to what is shown and what is not. Interpretation, after all, is never value-neutral, no matter how sincere the claims of impartiality. There is no innocent eye; reality is always read and written with prejudice, and maps are therefore susceptible to ideology and the abuse of power.[6] Powerfully effective symbolic and semantic effects of representation are found in the propaganda maps of Nazi Germany, for example, which presented geographical territories and figures in ways that were topographically incorrect in order to promote and control the nationalist imagination.[7] In less ominous ways, the maps of national parks, tourist areas, and commercial districts also precipitate forms of perception that serve the interests of those who commissioned the map. Similarly—in ways that are spatial, symbolic, and susceptible to misuse—the new aerial representations of the twentieth century have effected a new awareness of regional and global ecologies, instigated the planning and large-scale settlement of land, and colored the imaginations of millions of people who now live and act upon the planet.[8]

Changes in cultural practices and modes of understanding may precede or follow from innovations in representation. The development of pictorial perspective during the sixteenth century, for example, profoundly influenced the depiction of space as well as its subsequent design and construction, as infinitely extended lines radiated across the landscape and opened up the inward-looking enclosures of the medieval period. The gardens at Versailles exemplify perspectival practice, embodying a shift in spatial and aesthetic sensibility and at the same time symbolizing the new regal powers of seventeenth-century France together with the development of Enlightenment science.

For many artists, it is the inventive capacity of representation that enables them to provoke new and alternative ways of seeing the world. Similarly, the products of geographers, cartographers, historians, scientists, and writers enrich the cultural imagination and condition how and what actions are taken in the world. Black holes, DNA, the Bermuda Triangle, the equator, the desert, all these, like many other found places, are revelatory descriptions and constructions of reality. They are *ideas*. In turn, each of these new representations of the world becomes subject to the scrutiny of others, to be either corroborated and built upon or disagreed with and overturned. Further interpretations, instigated by and overlaid upon previous representations, shift and enrich a shared cultural reality with the passage of time. One must view with skepticism, then, those who claim to act upon the land with confidence and certainty (as might the "master-planner," for example), because such actions (measures) are always predicated upon a particular fiction, a representation (itself measured) that is not only ideologically loaded but also subject to shift and revision over time.

The enrichment of cultural life is predicated upon the continuing critical development of new modes of representation and interpretation, including that of the aerial view. Consider the walks taken by artist Richard Long, for example. These are first plotted as straight lines derived from an autonomous quantitative/geometric logic drawn across various maps. The subsequent walk along the line in the actual landscape reveals a series of unexpected collusions between map, land, and event, with each informing and challenging one another afresh.[9] An indifferent form of measured precision toward the dissection of map and land opens up a trajectory of completely unforeseen possibilities and events.

We hope that this intersection of document, method, and practice—of representation and inhabitation—will be evident in the photographs and map-drawings in this book, and that these illustrations will suggest alternative modes of seeing and acting upon America's evolving topography. We attempt to describe and to project upon the radically fictional nature of the American landscape, to quarry as well as to contribute to the accumulated layers of aerial representation and their agency of transformation. Perhaps our ultimate aspiration is that this work might provoke others who practice upon the land to see and act with a more critical, synoptic eye in the cultivation of future landscapes.

CHAPTER 3

THE AMERICAN LANDSCAPE AT WORK

A medium of ideas and imagination as much as of material substance, landscape pervades almost every aspect of daily life. As many American poets, painters, and filmmakers have recognized, the sublime omnipresence of the American landscape is difficult to escape. This pervasive quality derives not only from the sheer immensity and physical splendor of the land but also from the multitude of ways Americans have encountered, constructed, and represented it over time. These cultural processes, most often inspired and informed through direct engagement with the land, are also embodied in the workings of literature, painting, movies, and advertising. Consider, for example, the inseparable relationship between Thomas Cole's painting and the Hudson River Valley, or between Thoreau's writing and the New England woods, or—at a popular, subliminal level—between contemporary advertising images and the romanticization of postindustrial derelict landscapes. Thus, the results of inspired human effort and imagination, landscapes are not so much given as they are produced and subject to transformation.

One might be forgiven, however, for the assumption that America is a static, monotonous, and simplistic place, especially if only the repetitive rectilinearity of the middle-American landscape or the bland endlessness of suburbs are cited as examples.

But such viewpoints typically derive from a position outside those places, from looking at, rather than engaging with, the landscape. The same lines that delineate the repetitive grid are also fantastic corridors of movement, freedom, connection, diversity, and communication; the same bland suburban development is also home, family, community, and locus.[1]

Similarly, viewing the landscape from the altitude of a transcontinental flight does not allow a full understanding of the ongoing processes that give form to the land below or of how its appearance reflects human occupation and the day-to-day engagements involving people, land, material, and circumstance. Grids of interconnection, lines and arcs of pure circulation, endless circles and geometries of irrigation, cultivation, and abandonment; dams, mines, strip fields, silos, fields of windmills, hydroturbines, bomb test sites, airfields, radio-telescopes, levees, swales, woodlots, landfills, pilings, and plots of seemingly infinite dimension and possibility—this is a landscape at work, an infrastructure of pure productivity.

Linking this world of objects are transportation and distribution systems, communication networks, schedules, production lines, and other such measures of activity that make modern life as efficient and accessible as possible. Speed and availability collapse the physicality between space and distance, making the remote seem near and lending to the individual a sense of participation within national and global processes. Consequently, the American landscape ought to be valued less as a scenic and spatial phenomenon than as an active and temporal medium, the construction of

Cone of Iron Ore. Ashtabula, Ohio.

which is fluid, mobile, and transient. This is a medium of agents, networks, relationships, and representations, each unfolding with time. Those who claim to study the landscape objectively, as an isolated artifact or abstract system, delude themselves if they fail to recognize the shaping forces that continually act upon it.

The transmutative vibrancy of the working landscape reflects the American dream. The measure of what is moral and ideal for the American belongs less to the intellect than to the world of material action, to "getting the job done" bluntly, directly, and without pretension. Productivity and invention are, in turn, rewarded by material freedom, success, and wealth. Such is the American way, sustained by the effervescent buzz of material accumulation and the optimism of dreams.[2] The instruments and results of this material utility are inscribed all across the land, ceaselessly producing, circulating, consuming, moving, hauling, draining, transforming. With matter-of-fact directness, the American landscape presents itself as an immense expression of a pure and inexorable pragmatism that is spectacular in its banality, in its idealized realism, in its "actualization of utopia."[3]

What one sees from the air, then, are not merely attractive patterns and forms but great metabolic scaffoldings of material transformation, transmission, production, and consumption. The country is an enormous working quarry, an operational network of exchange, motion, and transmutation. Beyond its dramatic scenery, the American landscape is remarkable for the cultural activities and ideas that brought the country into being and that continue to diversify and effect its development; it is remarkable by virtue of its life in time, its *becoming*.

To appreciate the essential character of the American landscape, it is first necessary to understand how its appearance is an evolving expression of American ways of life and other material practices. To detach the landscape from culture as an object of scientific or aesthetic contemplation—to objectify it—is not only to fail to recognize the constitutive power of representation in the forming of reality but also to be distanced from the various reciprocities and indifferences that are structured between the land and its occupation by people.

Detail, plate 33.

CHAPTER 4

TAKING MEASURE
Irony and Contradiction in an Age of Precision

Immense and immediate. Efficient and wasteful. Brutal and spectacular. The American landscape, like the culture it embodies, is a magnificent paradox. For all of its clarity, beauty, and precision, there is an odd confusion lurking across the land, a terrifying and sweet errancy of measure that is at once ominous and promising. Poignantly expressed in all forms of social, economic, political, and aesthetic life, the grandeur of this irony is perhaps most concentrated in what I shall call the aporia of modern measure. This aporia is characterized by a general confusion of meaning and relationship between art and science, culture and nature, or objectivity and subjectivity. Our modern culture, particularly our relationship with the environment, is constructed upon dichotomies and oppositions that cannot seem to find a common measure.

I suggest that it is the absolute and calculative precision of modern measure—together with its claims of objectivity, rationality, and universality (claims that lend assurance to the production of empirical knowledge)—that underlies the current aporia, an aporia of aimless precision and entropic blandness that is made only more confusing, ironically, by virtue of the creativity and freedom it affords. I wish to assert at the outset that the mute efficiency of modern measure might also be its music, a silence at once discordant and magnificent. If so, then the aporia of modern measure, with all its irony and contradiction, might actually pre-

sent a situation that ought to be neither negated (as the poets and environmentalists may have it) nor affirmed (as the technocrats and engineers may believe) but, rather, critically appropriated and imaginatively redirected for its full, liberating promise to appear. One must accept and work to "deepen" the phenomenon of modern measure, while also turning it toward other sets of possibility and social purpose.[1]

Evidenced in many forms of social exchange, the aporia of modern measure is especially visible in the American landscape, the great crucible of spacing and geometry (from *geo*, meaning "earth," and *metry*, "measure"). On the surface, America is a carefully measured landscape of survey lines, rectangular fields, irrigated circles, highways, railroads, dams, levees, canals, revetments, pipelines, power plants, ports, military zones, and other such constructions. All are efficiently laid out with ingenious indifference to the land, crossing desert, forest, plain, marsh, and mountain with a cool, detached, and rational logic. These highly planned constructions are literally measures that have been taken across the American landscape in order to ensure a productive human occupation of the earth and its resources. Many of these measures possess dimensions precise yet fantastic, and they have constructed what is perhaps the closest approximation of utopia yet achieved by humankind. The United States has emerged over the past two centuries as a remarkably democratic and powerful nation, a land in which practically everything has become available and anything is now possible. In the words of Jean Baudrillard (who is preoccupied with the ambiguities and simu-

Detail, plate 117.

lacra of modern reality): "Everything here is real and pragmatic, and yet it is all the stuff of dreams too. . . . America is utopia made actual."[2] What appear to be some of the most prosaic and banal measures in the modern landscape (roads, transmission lines, and survey lines, for example) actually provide a "hyper-reality" of exhilarating and emancipating opportunity. Looking out across an infinite horizon, the dreams of Americans are inextricably bound into the utilitarian and material characteristics of the land (a relationship among land, labor, and hope that, curiously, was also true for premodern Native Americans, albeit of a radically different nature).

The paradox is not only of a dream reality, however. America is also a land of violence, indifference, and estrangement. Misfortune, stress, and fear are commonplace, symptoms of a "dis-measure" or a radical inequity and incongruity between things that comes as much from the land as from social conflict. Meteorological and geological disasters seem to occur with the same scale of extreme indifference as do crime, greed, and hate, for example. For all the generous provision that America's measures yield, the land remains a callous domain, a sprawling and vulgar monstrosity where many are made to feel disoriented and fearful. This America is a placeless space wherein all values are neutralized and all measures voided of meaning. Here is utopia's absolute antithesis, a dystopia of dreadful dimension.

There is, then, an inevitable ambivalence to modern life in America. Although the measures of American life liberate people from the confines of nature and ideological tyranny and grant access and opportunity to almost everyone, the same measures have also proven to be oddly inadequate and even onerous, especially in their destruction of ecological and social relationships. In spite of providing wealth, freedom, hope, and potential for millions of people, modern measures have been largely ineffective in alleviating fear, alienation, meaninglessness, pollution, and waste. It would appear that for every determination and provision of technological measure, there follows a peculiar excess or deficiency, as if everything becomes at once overly specific and overly simplistic. Consider the immense hydroengineering projects in the West, for example. Enormous dams, power plants, canals, and irrigation systems have made an arid landscape productive and home to millions of people; yet the long-term effects of salt and silt accumulation, loss of habitat diversity, and increased population demands commit this otherwise creative system to failure.

The failure of measures is not only environmental and economic but also social and ethical. For many people today, modern reality appears fragmented, temporary, and without great purpose. Within such a flux of discontinuity (both spatial and temporal), all that seems to matter is an eternal present, the here and now, with scant memory of what has gone before and little enthusiasm, hope, or responsibility for the future. Of course, that so many continue to find America utterly fascinating and liberating to live in (myself included) only compounds this extraordinary aporia, lending to it a good dose of irony. As expressed in the air-conditioned casinos and fountains of Las Vegas; in the irrigated lawns across the arid deserts of Arizona and southern California; on the freeways and interchanges; in the ubiquitous gas stations and parking lots; in the volume and diversity of foodstuffs grown on synthetically managed fields east, west, and central; or in the sprawling cities with their tall, corporate towers, peripheral ghettos, and green, bucolic suburbs, American life is extremely vibrant, exciting, productive, accessible, and desirable; yet at the same time it is all so strangely enslaved, entropic, meaningless, and monstrous.[3] Like a drug or hallucinogen, America is perhaps at once sweet and bitter, and nobody will give it up or want to see it go away. This double-edged paradox belongs uniquely to modern America, where heterogeneous and fragmented characteristics stand in stark contrast to the various structures of traditional societies and the more harmonizing role of measure in structuring their worlds.

Traditional Measures

Traditional measures possessed two characteristics that are no longer a part of modern convention. The first was the capacity of measure to relate the everyday world to the infinite and invisible dimensions of the universe, whether they be the movement of the planets, the rhythm of the seasons, or the actions of heavenly deities. For Plato, the definition of the good and the beautiful belonged to measure, appropriateness, and harmony. Ancient geometry, in particular, embodied cosmic order, symbolizing an ideal wholeness of relationship between the activities of people on earth while revealing the supreme order and perfection of the divine and universal. Nature and art were not antithetical but together revealed a wholesome and unified order.[4] Moreover, nature was understood as the ultimate source of beauty and held priority in the cosmography of many ancient cultures. Art and measure simply revealed the perfection of natural order and the supremacy of cosmic law, a unity that was also understood (in a different way) by Native American cultures such as the Hopi and the Anasazi and embodied in their cosmographic construction of space.

The second characteristic of traditional measure was its development through the relationship of the human body to physical activities and materials. In medieval Ukraine, for example, farmers would speak of a "day of field," referring to the area of land that they could physically sow or harvest in one day.[5] Obviously, the actual area would vary according to the lay of the land and the physical capacity of the individual farmer. Similarly, in early France, an *arpent* represented the area that a farmer could plow in one day using two oxen. Again, this measure, like other highly local and socially derived measures, varied greatly depending on circumstance. Fields along the west coast of Ireland, for example, were traditionally sized according to the distance a farmer was able to carry stones removed from the topsoil, a measure recorded today in the spacing between stone walls. These spacings and markings across the land, as with the farmer's calloused hands and crooked back, are visible measures of occupational circumstance; they are evolved forms of expression, the results of physical negotiation with the land, the elements, and the contingencies of a given situation.

Traditional units of measure therefore derived from the interrelationship of labor, body, and site. Tailors measured cloth using "arms" along its length and "hands" across its width, for example. Horses, too, were so many "hands" high, though this measure was not used with other animals. Similarly, a place a "stone's throw away" was not equal to one that was at "shouting distance." The sources of traditional measures were the concrete experiences of everyday life. Such measures were situated in the specific and were not necessarily applicable to other circumstances; they signified the value of a particular quantity along with its situational quality. An acre or a hectare, by contrast, quantifies an area into a standard unit but speaks not of its qualitative value or its circumstances of being.

The practical and place-specific nature of traditional measure, together with its idealized, cosmographic import via geometry, meant that the traditional world was generally conceived of as an organic whole, lending a representational and socially interactive unity to life (demonstrated in this book through the Hopi and Chacoan examples, pls. 102–113). Both the phenomenal and imaginative dimensions of reality were structured through these earlier uses of measure and geometry. Owing to the capacity of traditional measure to imbue practical life with symbolic meaning, such measures made coherent the relationships between people, place, activity, morality, and beauty.

Modern Measures

The socially and symbolically derived coherency of traditional measure began to change during the scientific revolution of the seventeenth century. Following the radical developments put forth by Galileo, Bacon, Newton, and Descartes, measure assumed an increasingly autonomous and self-referential place in human knowledge, becoming less and less connected to experiential and culturally situated origins. The Enlightenment philosophers severed, or abstracted, the world from the subject in order to dissect it for empirical study. The sterility and isotropic constancy of the modern laboratory ensured that things could be studied in isolation, without external interference. Thereafter, the world came to consist of an array of quantifiable and manipulable objects arranged in homogeneous and absolute space. No longer were things qualified by their relation to a specific subject, place, or situation; instead, the various "parts" of reality were objectified and rendered neutral. Consequently, measure developed into a radically autonomous practice, related not to the phenomenal and interactive world but to things as solitary and inert objects. This splitting of the objective from the subjective established, for the first time, a detached distance between the human and phenomenal worlds, enabling humankind to assume a position of supremacy and mastery over nature. Thus, the synoptic perspective of modern technology promoted detached forms of surveillance that enabled an unprecedented belief in the human ability to control the natural world and forge ahead with the building of utopia. Furthermore, the potential for interrelatedness between diverse things was broken (or at least suppressed) and is marked today in a number of incommensurate situations, such as the polarity between the "rationalism" of the engineer and the "sensibility" of the artist, between the instrumentality of technology and the phenomenology of dwelling, or between the life of the universe and the life of the individual.

Consider the modern period's definition of the meter, which was originally devised in France in 1799 as a unit equal to 1/40,000,000 of the earth's meridian.[6] Later, from 1889 to 1960, a single bar of platinum and iridium alloy was kept in a Parisian assay office as an internationally binding standard for the meter. To reduce the tolerance of inaccuracy, the meter has since been defined as "a length equal to 1,650,763.37 wave lengths of the orange light emitted by the Krypton atom of mass 86 in vacuo,"[7] a convention that was specified in the isotropic, dehumanized space of the laboratory. Thus, unlike the significant measures of the past, modern measures emerged as the outcome of technocratic convention; they have no greater social or cosmographic significance than the mathematical and international need for universal standards.

Unwittingly, the Enlightenment philosophers heralded a new technological era in which the universal application of measure was to become the ultimate instrument of human dominion, with the consequence that the world was reduced to a neutral stock of resources made available for profit and gain. This blinkered, detached form of measure is obviously significantly different from the qualitative, concrete, and symbolic types of traditional measure, yet these autonomous forms of measure underlie much of the development of the American landscape during the past two centuries and continue to pervade cultural reasoning today.

This brief account of modern measure is neither so clean-cut nor nihilistic in modern-day America, however. As suggested earlier, America is more of a paradox than it is a sterile, mute, and easily dissected object. Although modern measure has pervaded the making of the American landscape, it has, at the same time, exposed a richness inherent to technology when situated in the cultural context of the United States. Consider the case of Thomas Jefferson, who is credited with the early planning of the National Land Survey.

Detail, plate 61.

Modern Measures and
the American Landscape

For Jefferson, measure was not only of technological and instrumental value but also of moral and social worth. Beginning in his youth, Jefferson was constantly engaged with measuring, surveying, and map making. As evidenced in the interiors at Monticello, he surrounded himself with all sorts of measuring instruments—compasses, rulers, scales, sighting lenses, barometers, tripods, microscopes, tables, charts, transects, and the like. These allowed him to pursue his fascination with observing natural phenomena, especially the weather, the passage of the seasons, the forces of the environment, gardening, farming, and botany. In particular, he was interested in observing and recording their measurable characteristics, from which he derived numbers, patterns, laws, and rhythms. These measured findings were of great practical import, enabling him to invent and order things in a rational, accessible manner.

Jefferson was just as interested in modest everyday events as he was in national affairs and politics. One of his favorite vegetables, for example, was the pea, and he went to great lengths to study the cultivation and growth habits of this epicurean delight. He wrote: "[On February 20th] I sowed a bed of forwardest and a bed of midling peas. 500 of these peas weighed 3 oz . . . about 2,500 fill a pint; [March 19th] . . . both beds of peas up. . . . April 24th: forwardest of peas come to table. . . . Here, our first peas [are the] cheapest, pleasantest, and most wholesome part of comfortable living."[8] This busy and important man took the time to plant, cultivate, observe, measure, and savor the delights of such a minor vegetable! But, in so doing, Jefferson finds that it is the quantitative and analytical aspects of measure that enable "the most wholesome part of comfortable living." Although he is, of course, relating wholesome living to the refined cultivation of the pea, he is, by extension, also invoking what is good and beautiful in human dwelling. Through modesty, restraint, and measured

discipline, immeasurable delights are made possible. With neither waste nor excess, a harmonious relationship among a man, the vegetable world, and the graces of civilized dining might be said to have been structured through the rigors of modern measure. Numeracy, activity, and value are here linked in a form of purposeful and creative (admittedly modest) reciprocity.

Further, there are always moral and aesthetic judgments embodied within dimensions, quantities, and proportions for Jefferson. In criticizing the Capital at Williamsburg, for example, he wrote: "The Capital is a light and airy structure, with a portico in front of two orders, the lower of which, being Doric, is tolerably just in its proportions and ornaments, save only that the intercolonnations are too large. The upper is Ionic, much too small for that on which it is mounted and its ornaments not proper to the order, nor proportioned within themselves. It is crowned with a pediment which is too high for its span."[9] For Jefferson, what was "just" and "proper" was a matter not only of dimensional exactitude but also of aesthetic and social propriety. He inherited this understanding from the European tradition and put it into practice in the siting and architecture of his home at Monticello.

In conceiving of the National Land Survey, Jefferson was most concerned with making land available, efficiently and equitably, for purchase and ownership by individuals. During a number of debates on the procedures for the division, marking, and sale of land, Jefferson had a guiding imperative: that "as few as possible shall be without at least a little portion of land."[10] This vision was later worked into the Land Ordinance Act of 1785 and then revised as the Land Act in 1796, which was when the survey really began (the procedure having been altered from that first proposed by Jefferson, which used a different dimensioning system and did not account for the converging of north-south lines).[11] The measuring of the American landscape was therefore less about dominion and possession than it was about the democratic and legal sale of land and its subsequent settlement. Any person could own a piece of the American dream and share in its bounty.

The unit by which land was to be divided was called a Gunter's Chain, a standard surveyor's chain used in England that consisted of 4 perches, or rods, each 16½ feet long, making a chain equal to 66 feet. This unit proved useful because 10 square chains define an acre, and 640 acres fit into a square mile. Using repetitive survey procedures, the entire country was thereby marked according to a rectilinear grid following the lines of latitude and longitude.

To regulate the sale of land and avoid wholesale purchasing of large areas by land speculators, the government devised a system of division organized around thirty-six-square-mile "townships," defined by a square whose sides measured six miles, which was believed to be a reasonable distance for horse and wagon to get to market and back. These townships were in turn divided into thirty-six parcels measuring one square mile, called "sections." Sections were numbered in what was called "boustrophedonic order" (or as the plow follows the ox), a curious appropriation of a traditional procedure by a such a modern and rational scheme.[12] The sixteenth lot was typically reserved for community institutions and schools. Later, in order to make smaller parcels available to more people, sections were divided; first, into half sections, then quarter sections, then half-quarter and quarter-quarter sections. This latter unit is forty acres and was legislated into effect in 1836, and it remains the plot that is most evident in the Midwestern states today.

Needless to say, errors and adjustments were made during the survey and settlement of the land, some of which are illustrated later in the book. My main purpose here is to show how the measuring of land was itself a measure to ensure efficient, equitable, and secure occupancy by a free and hard-working people. Expressed in the form and pattern of this system is a major social imperative, one that reflects democratic and socially just proportion more than anthropocentric domination and autocratic control.

This latter view is perhaps understandable only in the context of the apparent indifference of those conducting the survey to local variations in topography, hydrology, and soils. One consequence of this bureaucratic inflexibility was that townships and individual lots sometimes differed in quality from neighboring plats. Moreover, the configuration and size of a piece of land were not necessarily the most appropriate given the ecosystem of a particular region (the drumlin and Finger Lakes region of upper New York state, for example; pls. 16, 17) or particular types of occupancy (American Indians could make no sense or use of the grid, and hillside farmers found the rectilinear property lines too awkward for plowing their sloped fields efficiently; pls. 10, 11).

The French method of land division on the American continent was, by contrast, more responsive to its physiographic context (pls. 20, 21). Most settlement by the French occurred along river floodplains (especially great arterial rivers such as the Mississippi and the St. Lawrence) owing to their interest in using these trade corridors to ship goods (especially furs) back to Europe during the seventeenth and early eighteenth centuries. In response to the meandering nature of the river and the need of settlers to have their own access to the river frontage, straight lines were drawn perpendicularly to the river's edge to delineate property parcels, or long-lots. Each long-lot had a river frontage of two to three arpents (384 to 576 feet) and was typically ten times as long as its width.[13] Because each occupant had access to the river, the fertile floodplain soils, and the higher protected land at the end of the lot, they all shared the benefits and dangers of settling along the river. Such adjustment of land division to physiographic and programmatic circumstance was, of course, common to other forms of settlement (such as New England villages and hillside towns) prior to the development of the more direct and regularized procedures of the National Land Survey.

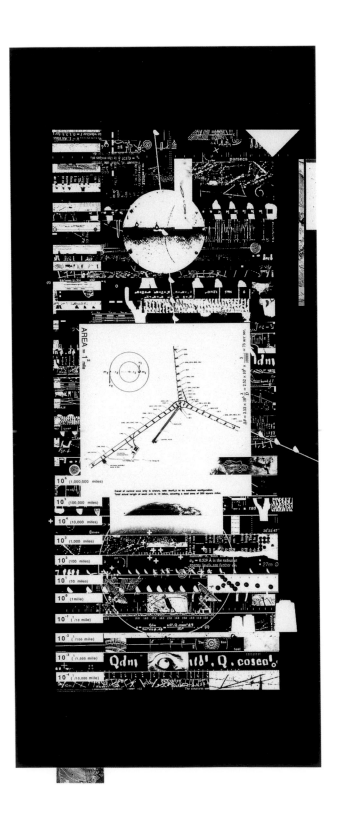

Qualitative Determination

Questions of survey, inventory, number, size, scale, spacing, and interval continue to surface in the present-day planning and design of land. How these spatial determinations are made, however, is not so easy to answer. How does one know, in fact, the correctness and propriety of a particular spatial or material judgment? From where do these measures derive? More often than not, it appears that certain technical standards, as documented in manuals and technical guidebooks, serve as the benchmark for contemporary dimensioning and apportioning. Some land planners speak of "determinants," or quantifiable factors, that lead logically to certain measures and solutions. In fact, the modern production of environments by engineering and landscape-architectural professionals is becoming increasingly standardized owing to the capacity of computers to store and manipulate all of the "determinant variables" and "prototypical solutions" for a given problem. The material world is subsequently spaced and organized according to some standardized specification that is usually required by warranty or legal code. To build anything less would be irresponsible with respect to the "health, safety, and welfare" of the "public" (whoever that constituency actually is), and to do anything more would be gratuitous (at least according to the often-anonymous makers of these rule books).

Moreover, there is little uncertainty as to the success of these norms; they are at least sufficient for most situations. The result, of course, is a ubiquitous and standardized built environment, one that looks the same in New York as it does in Anchorage or Albuquerque. The experience and challenge of spatial discovery

Powers of Ten II. Very Large Array Radio Telescope, Magdalena, New Mexico, 14 × 20".

are consequently impoverished, with differences blended into the lowest common denominator and finally eradicated. Every place, regardless of special characteristics, begins to look and feel alike— neutral, flat, and bland.

Fortunately, there are some aspects of the environment that, as yet, have not been subject to the rigor (mortis) of standardization. For example, some of the best landscape architects I know have expressed anxiety when making spatial and programmatic determinations in design. One struggles over the spacing of a grove of poplar trees in a particular place: should they be fifteen, eighteen, or twenty feet on center? Another never seems confident that the slope of a hill be graded one in four (the ratio of the vertical fall to the horizontal dimension); perhaps it should be one in five, one in six, or even one in eight. Others take pains over the dimensions of a wall or step, sizing them differently every time owing to the uniqueness of a given situation. Each of these designers struggles with standards and norms because each has his or her own sense of how something ought to be in a particular circumstance. They decide how big or how small a designed element should be, without a ruler in hand or a particular program in mind. They decide that a certain material is too warm or too cold without thermometer or reference to radiant temperature. Instead, these spatial and material determinations are qualitatively negotiated; they are the outcome of informed experience and the "feeling out" of those phenomena believed to be most appropriate given the circumstances. Consequently, their designs are impossible to replicate elsewhere without their becoming somehow unfitting or improper. Informed by judgments about what is correct for a given situation, the measures taken by these designers are best approximations rather than certainties. As such, they derive from a culturally grounded form of accuracy, a qualitative precision that is quite different from that of the technomathematical. Like Michelangelo's "false truths" (those artistic representations that appear to be more correct in feeling and in truth of spirit than the "true falsehoods" of empirical quantification), such intuitive determinations of measure are always peculiar to and right for their contextual circumstance.[14] Through their inventive fitting, such measures might also be understood in terms of metaphor in that their span reaches to join and produce something new.

What we may learn from this sense of qualitative precision is that quantities, limits, spacings, and tolerances are always situated within a complex milieu of social, moral, and aesthetic implications. To cite Jacques Derrida: "We appear to ourselves only through an experience of spacing. . . . What happens through [this spacing] both constructs and instructs [who we are]."[15] To gauge and space the world is not only to reflect upon the nature of human existence on earth but also to construct a relationship among people, community, and environment. By extension, to exercise "good measure" in everyday life is to practice what feels right and proper, with precision, economy, and grace. Measured correctness, then, is less of dimensional, mathematical exactitude than it is of moral propriety and precision of judgment—attributes that are culturally acquired and practiced within given circumstances; they cannot be practiced using the codes and conventions of standards and norms. As such, measure guides interpretation and action in ways that are as much qualitative and situated as they are quantitative and universal. This is more a practical form of knowledge than a strictly theoretical mode of knowing. It is the present-day incongruity, however, between these two conditions—between the instrumental, calculative, objective, standardized, and formulaic, on the one hand, and the sensual, poetic, subjective, and contingent, on the other—that I see as characterizing the aporia of measure in late twentieth-century America. As I stated at the outset, I believe that neither position (the traditional or the modern) should be privileged over the other but, rather, that both need to be brought into a greater form of reciprocity.

The Reconciliatory Function of Measure

In a short, beautiful essay entitled ". . . Poetically Man Dwells. . . ," Martin Heidegger reflects upon the essential nature of measure. Drawing from the poetry of Friedrich Hölderlin, Heidegger proclaims that "the taking of measure is what is poetic in dwelling."[16] He later turns this phrase around to read: "In poetry there takes place what all measuring is in the ground of its being."[17]

How are we to understand this elusive claim? Perhaps one must live in the poetic before any clear understanding is possible. The musician or the poet may not find such a claim elusive, perhaps appreciating the fact that Heidegger cannot be more explicit in grounding these assertions than through analogical reasoning. Almost certainly, he is not speaking of the quantitative and the instrumental here; after all, the dimensions and weights of the material world have been measured over and over again, from the scale of the solar system to that of the genetic code, and yet all of these data ultimately remain prosaic and flat. Moreover, sophisticated legislative and concrete measures have been taken across the surface of the earth, and well beyond. Perhaps at no other time have so many varied and complex measures been taken than during the twentieth century, and yet is it really possible to say that Americans "dwell poetically" today? Has there developed an authentic level of reciprocity among individuals, social communities, and the natural world? Whereas poetry and art are readily available to modern culture, this provision does not seem to be sufficient evidence of a "poetic society." In fact, if homelessness, pollution, waste, withdrawal, and general estrangement are to serve as guides, the dwelling of modern culture is altogether unpoetic, brutally real and entropic. Ironically, these same social conditions have also been subject to enormous efforts of measurement by government and scientific agencies, to little avail.

Heidegger, too, recognizes these characteristics of modern life. In fact, he suggests that "our unpoetic dwelling, [our] incapacity to take the measure, derives from a curious excess of frantic measuring and calculating."[18] This excess is likened to the person who cannot see simply because he sees too much—a situation that is exemplified in the way measures of technoeconomic exigency tend to overspecify and oversimplify at the same time, dominating and rendering trivial other forms of seeing and acting in the modern world. The result is an atrophy in the health and diversity of the biosphere and of culture, characteristic of late twentieth-century life. As documented by natural and social scientists alike, this deterioration has aesthetic and experiential effects (as evidenced in the increased homogeneity and impoverished state of the environment), together with ecological and ethical implications (such as the anthropocentric will to power over all others and the diminishing of alterity and difference).

Clearly, the measure taking of which Heidegger and the poets speak differs from the purely calculative and instrumental. It is a measure taking that is about the "letting appear" of what is right and fitting in human existence. This reconciliation of opposites is what is revealed by the poetic measure, the metaphor. Such measures are good and beautiful in their spanning and joining of differences, connecting things to make possible more wholesome forms of existence. As Albert Hofstadter comments: "Man's measure is not a quantity that can be calculated. Only man's being itself can tell what its measure is, by the fiery test of the living encounter of the human self with reality. . . . Human measure is to be sought in the quantity of our belonging—in the magnitude, direction, and degree of our being with the other as with our own."[19] The kind of interconnectivity spoken of here is one of relationship, a spatiotemporal mode of being among others in circumstantial and reciprocal ways.

Detail, plate 97.

Measures as metaphors might therefore be said to increase the world's being, further diversifying and enriching one thing's life among a multitude of others, which is ultimately of both ecological and social value.[20]

A further understanding of this reconciliatory function of measure need not be obscure or theoretical, for people practice good and just measure in daily life. When one enters into a conversation, participates in a dance, or sits to eat with friends, a sense of what constitutes appropriate behavior and response prevails. In philosophical terms, this self-awareness of measure is called "practical wisdom": one is conscious of the quantities, properties, and limits of one's being within a particular circumstance, and is aware of how to extend and foster kinship with others.[21] By extending oneself with due measure (which is what ensues in any conversation or dance), one overcomes separation and distance to construct relationship and dialogue. These social measures unite self with other. With respect to the earth, such relationships are the foundations for culturally wholesome forms of cultivation and dwelling; they structure a spatial and ethical "fittingness" between the natural and social worlds that is neither excessive nor wasteful.

Obviously, humility and temperance pervade such an ethic. Measured behavior, for example, implies a sense of restraint and awareness of one's measure with respect to an-other. As defined by Hofstadter: "Temperance is the keeping to due measure and proportion in the things that concern us—appetites, desires, aspirations, and claims; by our temperance we stay within the bounds of what belongs to us; we do not exceed the measures assigned to us by the nature of our being."[22] When one does exceed these limits ("by mete and bound") there typically follows a sense of separation and lostness, characterized by such conditions as loneliness, addiction, obsession, schizophrenia, madness, alienation, and social withdrawal.

Here, then, lies the heart of the aporia of modern measure, with all of its irony and contradiction. In an age of precision and advanced technological resources, people are at once closer to and more estranged from the earth and one another. On the one hand, standard and universal measures—each mathematically precise beyond any perceptible tolerance of magnitude—have fostered global cooperation and mutual understanding, thereby diminishing the threat of despotic tyranny and misrepresentation while providing new and advanced forms of medicine, communication, and technology. On the other hand, both the uniqueness and relatedness of things and places are objectified and diminished through modern measures, promoting forms of homogeneity and alienation. Just as overspecification and oversimplification are the results of modern measure, so too are freedom and constraint, accessibility and estrangement. Could not this same dichotomy apply to American society and its landscape, wherein all that is generous, extending, and creative is both enabled and constrained by a universal, autonomous system? Certainly this is what lends irony to the "hydraulic society" of the Southwest, for example.[23]

Of course, the reverse of this situation is that the abstract systems of technology are both resisted and absorbed by prevailing social, cultural, and natural realities. Technological measure itself has no home; it is autonomous and freewheeling. Yet, when applied, it must always touch down somewhere at some time and must therefore become engaged with the wild forces of place and time. Here, the system will inevitably yield, further thickening and evolving the quarry of cultural and biological life.[24] For example, for all of its assumed monotony, the National Survey Landscape is incredibly rich and diverse when experienced firsthand; the land, the passages of time, and the peculiarities of subsequent settlements have resisted and absorbed the ideality of the rational and repetitive scheme—a scheme that, in fact, facilitated fair and accessible opportunity for democratic settlement and land ownership.[25] Although there are places where lines do not quite meet up, where roads are not straight or true, where property lines take strange and irregular turns, and where the rectilinear order breaks down, it is the system that bends—albeit unwillingly and with little grace. Still, the point is that everyday life upon the land has evolved a rich and delirious landscape, a complex imbroglio of farmsteads, diners, gas stations, crop dusters, motels, floods, tornadoes, baseball, cornfields, towns, hillsides, plains, conversations, arguments, dances, sunrise, snow, and drought. This same richness, accrued through a kind of earthbound and inevitable errancy, might also describe other technological constructions upon the land. BIOSPHERE II, in Arizona, for example, is a completely sealed and self-sustaining environment, a mathematically modeled container that continues to fail owing to its incapacity to allow for human desire, error, mischief, and change. Similarly, most urban design plans have failed in the twentieth century precisely because of this suppression of the volatile, the complex, and the unpatrollable, promiscuous forces of the city. The techniques, the measures, of contemporary urban and landscape design are simply incongruent to their object. As shown in the controlled environment of BIOSPHERE II, *life* cannot be created in the laboratory.

The work documented in this book represents a few initial explorations into this paradox of contemporary measures, some of which are lyrical, some banal. Revealed is the absurd and magnificent ingenuity of American people, a people enmeshed with yet remote from their land. Future work upon this ambiguously precise landscape might require a fresh approach toward how measure is deployed in landscape-architectural planning and design. More imaginative practices of measure and geometry than those of the calculative and instrumental must first be developed if modern culture is to construct a landscape that is truly fitting of social and ecological life. Such an understanding may be predicated increasingly upon the metaphoricity of measure, its ability to span and join across distance and time. In this approach, landscape and nature would shed their status as objects, as things possessed by measure, and emerge as active agents in the unfolding of life and in the relating of one to an-other. As with genes and ideas, such actants would be as playful and indeterminate as they would be precise and highly structured. Only then might the taking of measure assume further dimensions to those of either the traditional or the modern—dimensions of the precisely errant and the systematically bewildering.[26]

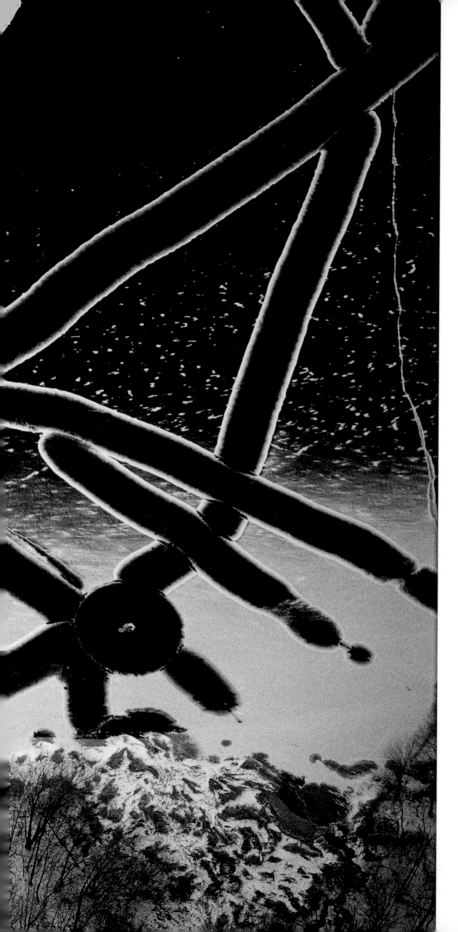

Part Two

MEASURES

Cracked Ice on Pond. Brockton, Massachusetts.

CHAPTER 5

MEASURES OF LAND

Measure is intrinsic to the design, habitation, and representation of land. It underlies the variety of ways land is traversed and negotiated; it enables the spacing, marking, delineation, and occupation of a given terrain; and it reflects the values and judgments of the society that live upon the land. Whether for purposes of navigation, cultivation, protection, or security, measure is taken to orient a particular reality, guiding a society's relationship to the land qualitatively as well as quantitatively. Measure, then, is as much a conceptual apparatus as it is a mode of representation, facilitating events while constructing a particular cultural world.

The immensity of the American landscape presented a challenge to the masses that came to America during the seventeenth and eighteenth centuries. Surveys, inventories, and maps had to be prepared, dimensions and areas determined, and areas of land marked and allotted for particular uses. All of this had to happen quickly. Many settlers were concerned with rights of ownership, hoping to avoid disputes over land rights and to prevent large areas of land from being bought by wealthy land barons on speculation and later sold at exorbitant prices.

As a result of the Land Ordinance Act of 1785, together with later National Lands Acts, the United States has today been cleared and radically transformed. Survey lines, roads, hedgerows, fences, farms, canals, levees, dams, bridges, buildings, and towns have been laid out as means of optimizing human settlement and opportunity. Embodied in the resultant spacings, tolerances, and limits of this national landscape are uniquely American values of democracy, freedom, accessibility, and social improvement.

It is fortunate, however, that the land itself has a way of both resisting and absorbing the systematic overlay of any survey. The land possesses its own measure that ultimately exceeds and confounds the modern measure taker. The land is like an immense crucible in which the processes of nature and the peculiar events of social exchange interact over time with unpredictable effects. Owing to the uncontrollable processes of life, the intended objectivity of pure quanta will always remain abstract and incomplete.

There is some irony, then, to the fact that measures of land are the means by which an environment—one that was once so strange and unknown—reveals itself, for what we actually find is only an illusion of human order, a screen behind which lies the unceasing cry of the wild.

Detail, plate 14.

1. *Stone Walls Overgrown by Forest.* Westerly, Rhode Island.

2. *Abandoned Homestead.* Eastern Washington. Many pioneer homesteaders traveled west in search of land that would be favorable for farming and raising a family. Upon finding a suitable area, they would settle and construct a homestead, a spatial complex that attached the family to an otherwise undifferentiated terrain. Often remote, these anchors of family life marked a steadfast place, an orienting locus in an endless landscape of unpredictability and danger.[1]

3. *Square-Lot Homestead.* Fargo area, North Dakota. The later homesteads that evolved as part of the National Land Survey (and especially after the Homestead Act of 1862) were spaced with regular repetition, knitting a geometric matrix of occupancy across the land. Today, these dwellings are typically enclosed by dense, rectangular woodlots rising above the flat plain as volumetric projections of a squared landscape. These plantings provide wood for fuel and protection from the ferocious winter winds, enveloping the family like a womb and marking an otherwise empty horizon.[2]

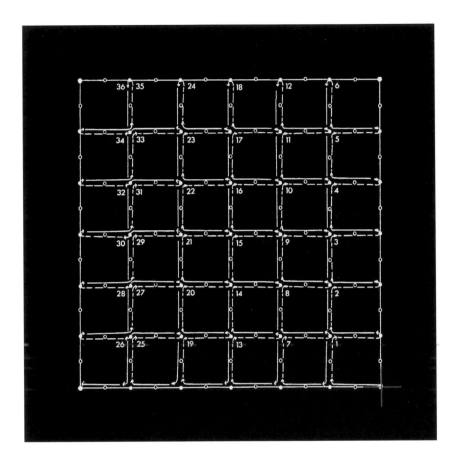

4. *Township Plat of Thirty-six Sections.* 14 × 20". Legislative and dimensional measures of lands west of the Alleghenies were first enacted through the Land Ordinance Act of 1785. Survey teams were sent out along the parallels to record the land and divide it into a grid of 36-square-mile townships. In turn, each township was divided into 1-square-mile units called sections. The sequential procedure for marking and numbering each section was done in "boustrophedonic order," or as the plow follows the ox.[3]

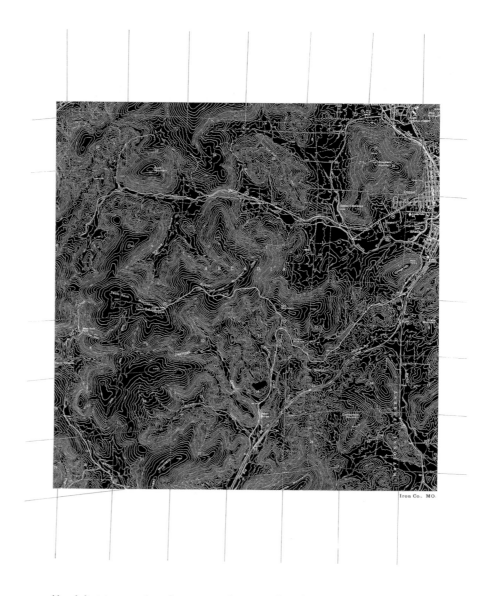

5. *Stray Survey Lines.* Ironton, Missouri. 14 × 20″. The entire system of land division was based on square, horizontal, and perpendicular relationships. The varying topography and curvature of the earth, therefore, proved troublesome for surveyors and legislators alike. Moreover, in the Ozark Mountains of Missouri, iron-ore deposits caused major deviations in magnetic compass readings that led to broken, disconnected, and straying grid lines.

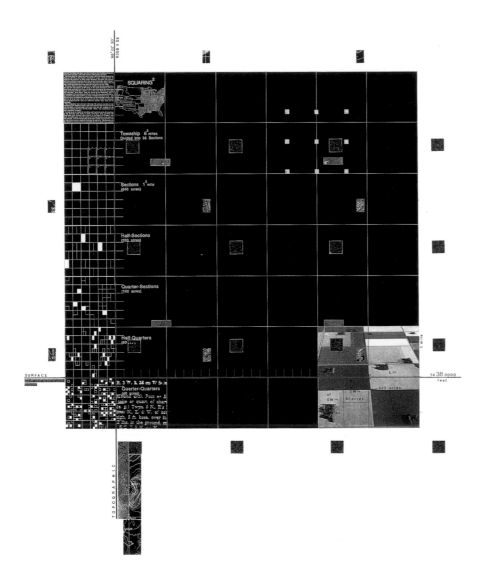

6. *The Survey Landscape.* 14 × 20″. To provide more people with the opportunity to purchase land, sections were later subdivided into half sections, quarter sections, half-quarter sections, and (after 1836) quarter-quarter sections, which is the forty-acre parcel most evident in the Midwest today. Section lines became roads and smaller plots of land were delineated and marked by posts and fences.

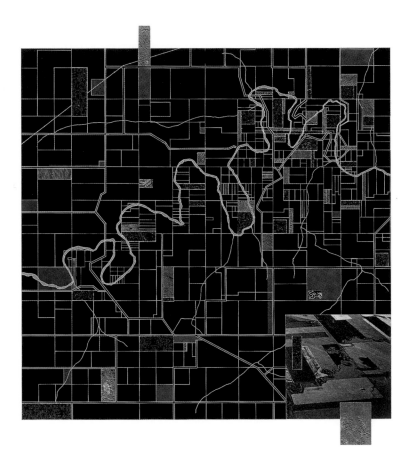

7. *The Survey Landscape Accrued.* 14 × 20". Although the application of the survey was mechanical and repetitious, a great deal of variety in the landscape has evolved over time. Local changes in topography, drainage, and soils have led to regional variation, as have presurvey patterns of settlement, Indian cessions, and other historical land rights that the surveyors had to bypass or negotiate. Also, parcelization varies, with some land owners occupying a full section, others a quarter section, and others a quarter-quarter section. In turn, woodlots, homesteads, enclosures, and patterns of cultivation differ, lending complexity to a simple and neutral geometry.

8. *The Survey Landscape from the Air.* Castleton, North Dakota. The rectilinear pattern of the survey literally constructs the isolationism of the American individual, providing for independent plots while hindering the development of linear or agglomerative communities (along roads and intersections, for example). Homesteads are instead spaced apart like atomized particles, fixed in space through geometric, equidistant repetition.

9. (opposite) *The Survey Landscape.* Castleton, North Dakota. The resultant survey landscape reflects a remarkably democratic mode of land settlement and ownership, one without hierarchy, prejudice, center, or limit.

10. *Remnant Beach Ridges across the Grid.* Reynolds, North Dakota. Ridges of old beach deposits from the receding edge of an ancient lake drift counter to the geometry of the survey grid in North Dakota. The variation in water-holding capacity, fertility, and slope of these residual soils, the result of particular topographical and hydropedological histories, demands a negotiated manner of farming overlaid upon the grid.

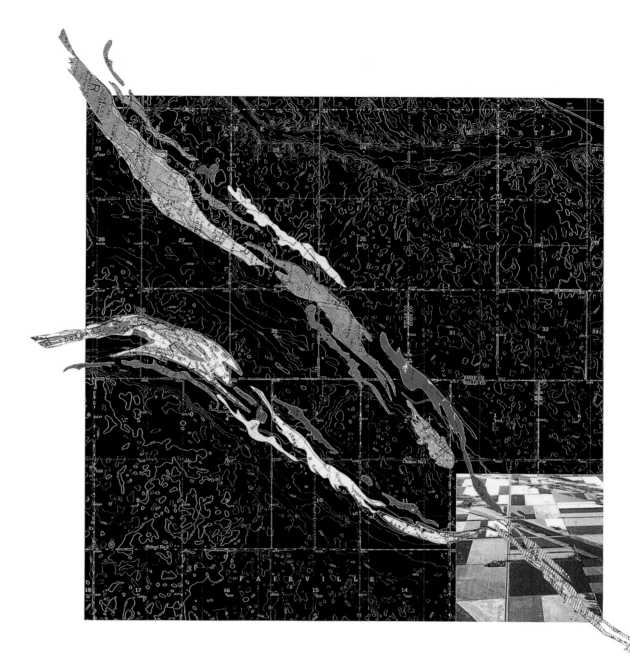

11. *Pedological Drift.* Fairville, North Dakota. 14 × 20".

12. *Railroads across the Survey Landscape.* Castleton, North Dakota. In the Northern Plain states, trains run along their own trajectories and gradients, indifferent to the repetition of the survey grid. Towns are often established along the railroad, sometimes as regularly as every six miles—a negotiated measure of rail friction reached between the grain farmers (who wanted more stops) and the railroads (who wanted fewer).

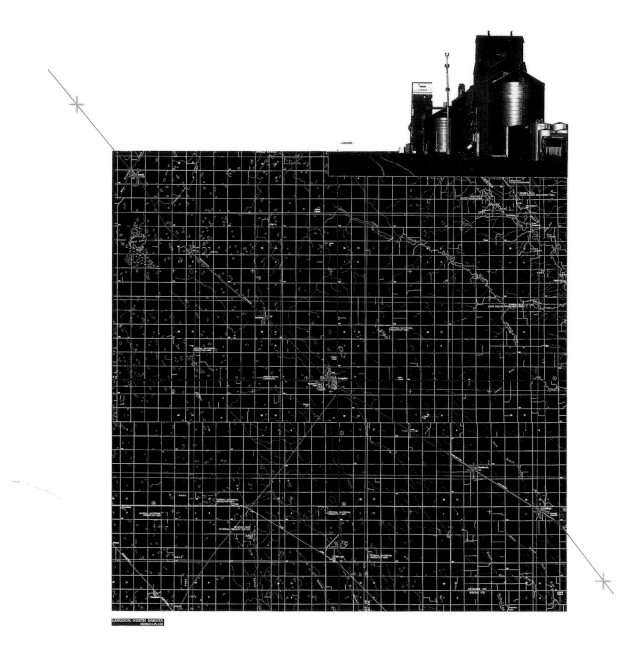

13. *Railroads across the Northern Plains.* 14 × 20″.

14. *Road Grid Correction Jog.* Castleton, North Dakota. It did not take long for legislators to understand that a township could not be exactly six miles on each side if the north-south lines were to follow the lines of longitude, which converged, or narrowed, to the north. The grid was, therefore, corrected every four townships to maintain equal allocations of land. These slippages, measured every twenty-four miles (or every thirty minutes if one was driving), poignantly register the spherical and magnetic condition of our planet, doglegging to counter the diminishing distances as one moves north.[4]

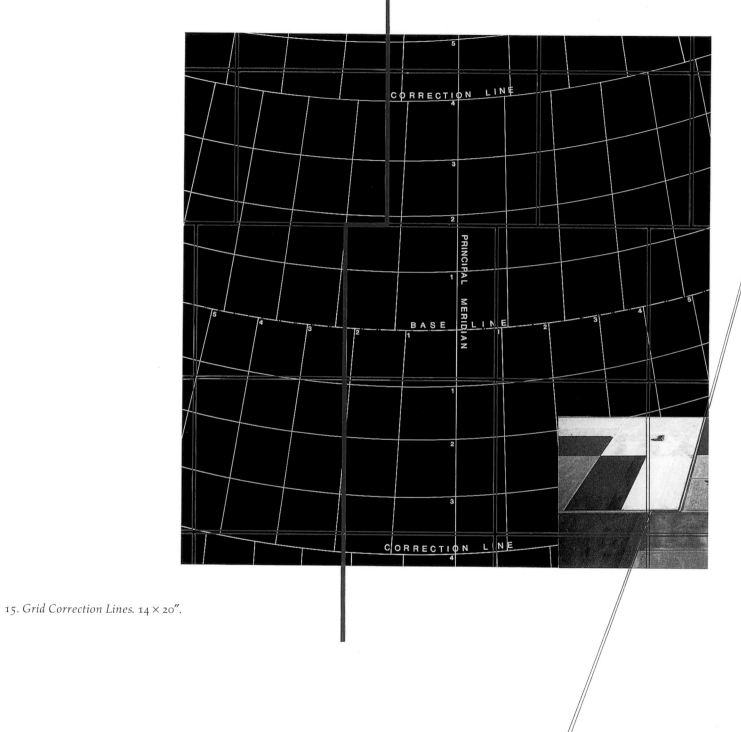

15. *Grid Correction Lines.* 14 × 20".

16. *Drumlin Settlement.* Williamson, New York. During the Wisconsin ice age some twenty thousand years ago, ice sheets extended as far south as southern Ohio. One of the many vestiges of this glacial activity was the deposition and shaping of drumlin fields around the Finger Lakes region of New York State. Drumlins are low, elongated hills that are composed from glacial till and trend in the same direction as the ice flow.

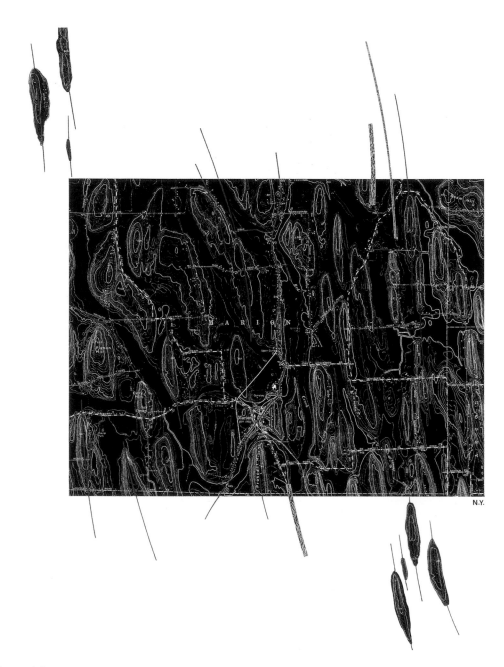

17. *Drumlin Fields*. Williamson, New York. 12 × 16″. Settlers and farmers were coerced by this topography to lay out roads and settlements along the gentler slopes, mirroring the direction of the glacier and disregarding the rectilinear delineations of the National Survey.

18. *Appalachian Linear Settlement.* Lykens, Pennsylvania. The Appalachian Mountains, which run from Maine to Tennessee as a uniform series of parallel ridges, were formed when the ancient continents of Laurentia, Gondwonaland, and Baltica were compressed nearly 500 million years ago. Richly veined with minerals and coal deposits, the Appalachians attracted mining communities during the nineteenth century. Towns were laid out in narrow lines along the valley floor, which was then cleared for farming and pasture. The forest line along the toe of the slope registers the edge at which gradients are too steep and soils too thin for fields.

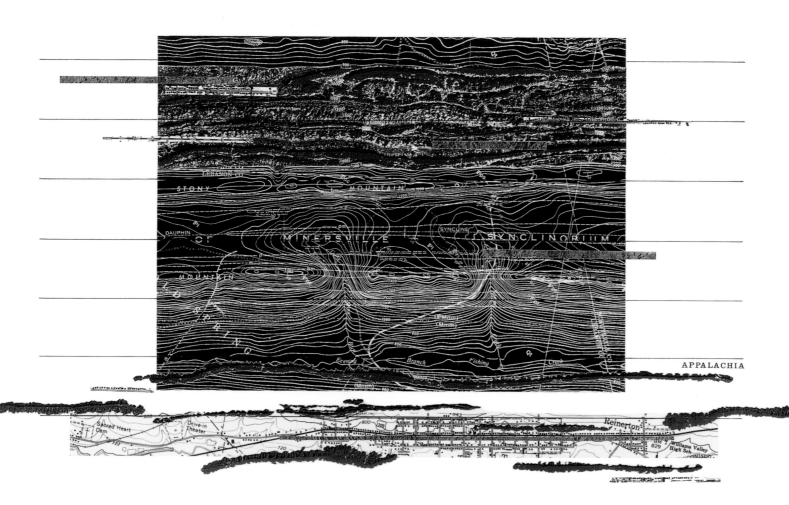

19. *Appalachian Ridge and Valley*. Central Pennsylvania. 12 × 16″. Coal was strip-mined along linear beds on the hillsides, the open cuts running in the same direction as the geologic and settlement patterns. Scars and derelict quarries remain today as evidence of exhaustion, both of human bodies and of geologic seams. Linear roads trace the center of the valleys, connecting the various towns. On occasion, the roads jump across to neighboring valleys through gaps cut in the ridge lines by rivers.

20. *Mississippi Long-Lots*. Hermitage, Louisiana. Early French settlers penetrated America along its waterways, especially the St. Lawrence and Mississippi Rivers, the country's largest arteries. Rivers became the primary organizing lines for subsequent settlement, which was plotted to run in long-lots perpendicular to the river's edge. Homes were therefore close together, often forming linear villages along the roads that followed the riverbanks.[5]

21. *Long-Lots along the Mississippi River.* Ascension Parish, Louisiana. 12 × 16″. Democratic and equitable, each inhabitant receives an equal share of river frontage, rich alluvial soils on the floodplain, and higher ground upon which to retreat during flood. Each shares equally in the riches and risks of settling upon the shifting floodplain.

22. *Desert Grid.* Mojave Desert, California. Traces of the survey grid, typically built as roads, are sketched into the ground of even the most inhospitable of places.

23. (opposite) *Desert-Oasis Housing Development.* Mojave Desert, California. The image of the detached, private home endures in much of the American cultural imagination. The grid, softened and curved a little, remains the geometry of choice, and emblems of paradise—water and trees—are artificially maintained within clearly bounded enclosures. What is outside remains precisely that—outside, without measure or influence upon the shaping of settlement.

24. *Ghost Development Plot.* Near Santa Fe, New Mexico. Sometimes, a template of roads can be seen on the desert floor, an image that deceives faraway investors into believing that their plot of land is real and available. When the new owners turn up to build their house, however, they find just another scam, measured from greed, foolishness, and mistaken dreams.

25. *Earthworks for Hillside Housing.* Near Los Angeles, California. The demand for the single house continues, forcing cities to expand their development into increasingly forbidding territory. In the foothills of Los Angeles, sudden rainfall and spring floods can cause enormous mud- and landslides, carrying development downhill and into ruin. Nonetheless, the engineering establishment continues to believe that it can control nature—in this case, by constructing stepped terraces.

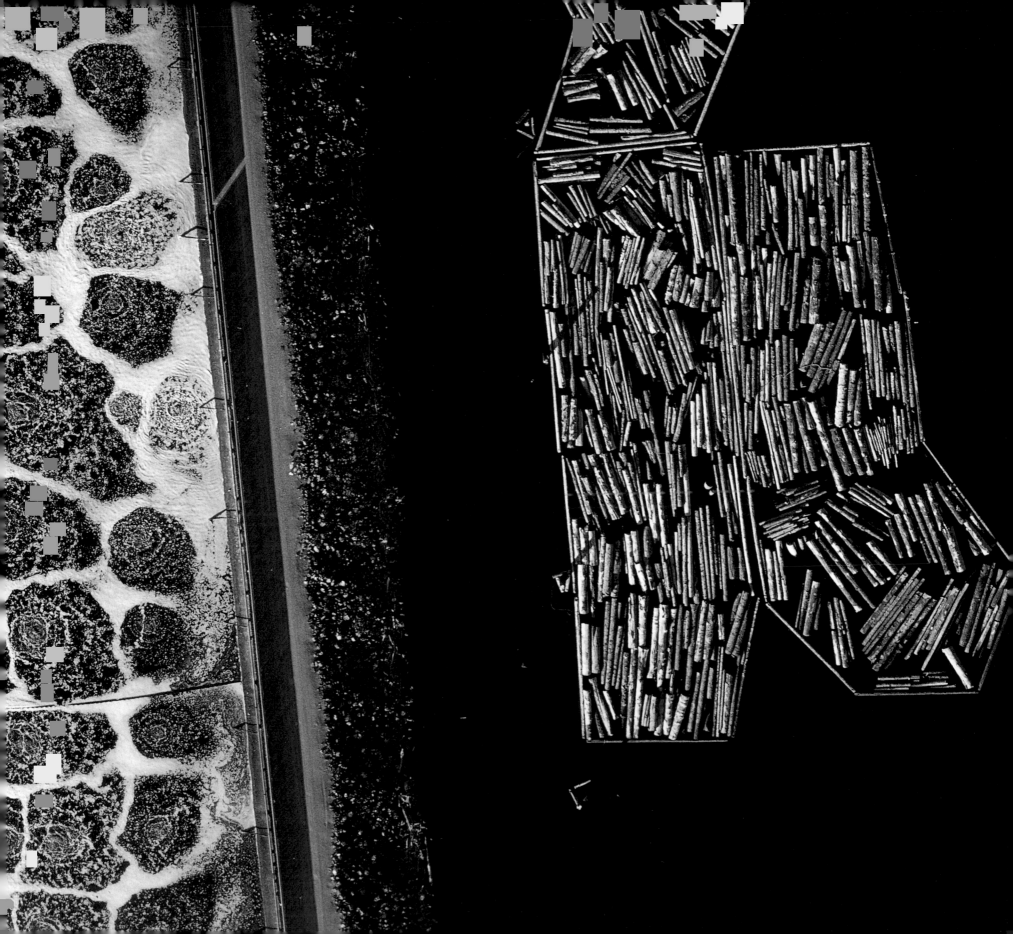

CHAPTER 6

MEASURES OF CONTROL

Measures facilitate possession. They enable one to occupy, control, and manipulate the land. Measures of control usually consist of a series of steps that are precautionary and of practical necessity, often in response to social and environmental exigencies.

The National Land Survey, which facilitated federal control over the land while assuring individual property rights, was one such measure. There are, however, many other measures in the landscape that characterize modern humankind's will to power, for example, the huge dams and hydroengineering projects, vast irrigation systems, communication and transportation networks, flood-control programs, energy-generating plants, transmission lines, and other such technological constructions found all across America.[1] From the air, the American landscape resembles an immense construction site of mechanisms and instruments, each working to optimize efficiency and utility. These measures not only facilitate modern life but also construct the environment in which we live.

Ironically, although numbers and efficiencies rarely approach poetic dimensions, they can often produce some of the most fantastic landscapes, creating a sublimity that is at once terrifying and immeasurable. This "awe-fullness" derives from the sheer autonomy of the technological measure, the ruthless indifference of which can be matched only by nature itself.[2]

Detail, plate 49.

26. *Forest Clear-Cut.* Northern Maine.

27. *Glen Canyon Dam*. Colorado River, Arizona. The spring snowmelts of the Colorado River watershed, high in the Rocky Mountains, cause the torrential flows of water that have formed the great canyons of Utah and Arizona. Today, this great water volume is controlled by a series of huge concrete dams that store the water in enormous lakes. Once-raging river ravines and deep valleys are now filled with passive water reservoirs, and the mouth of the great Colorado has been reduced to a trickle.[3]

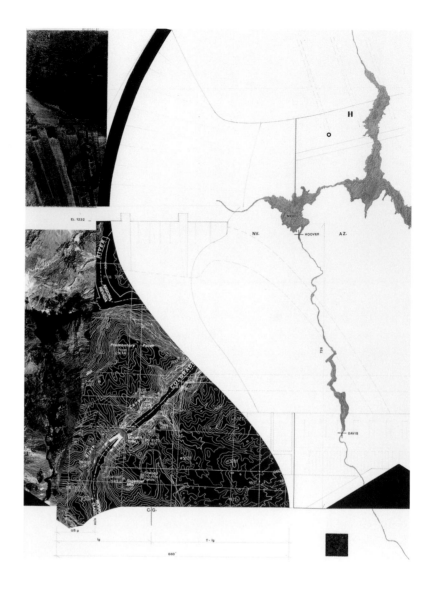

28. *Hoover Dam and the Colorado River.* Nevada. 14 × 20". Detailed calculations account for the release and distribution of each gallon of water along the Colorado. The dam, along with other measures along the river, provides water for crop irrigation, domestic use, and hydroelectric power in Nevada, Arizona, and California. Lake Mead, the reservoir for Hoover Dam, serves as storage for 9.2 trillion gallons of water (equal to nearly two years of the river's flow), which would cover Connecticut to a depth of ten feet.

29. Canal from the Colorado River. West of Phoenix, Arizona.

30. *Irrigation Canal and Rose Fields.* Bakersfield, California. Although irrigation continues to allow for the productive use of cropland, its continual recycling of water is increasing salt levels to such a degree that the water will soon become toxic for plants and unpalatable for humans.

31. *Citrus Groves with Sprinkler Irrigation*. Blythe, California.

32. (opposite) *Sprinkler Fields*. Blythe, California.

33. *Bay Channel with Transmission Lines.* Fremont, California.

34. *Solar Furnace.* Barstow, California. Rotating mirrors reflect and concentrate sunlight onto a furnace in the center of a circular field.

35. *Drainage Dikes along Roadside.* Phoenix, Arizona. Storms, snowmelt, and floods can occur with ferocious power in the deserts of the Southwest, washing away tons of surface material in a matter of minutes. Here, a series of massive dike structures are cut into the desert floor to help gather and channel these sheets of water, directing them beneath and away from the highway.

36. *Revetments along the Missouri River.* Missouri. On the outer bends of large rivers, water velocity increases and causes bank erosion. Eventually the meander of the river eats away at the bank. To protect farmland and property, occupants along the Missouri River have constructed long revetments perpendicular to the bank to slow the water. Not only is erosion curbed, but the decreased velocity causes the river to deposit sediment on the downstream side of the revetment (with the unfortunate result that erosion farther downstream is typically increased).

37. *Windmills along Ridge Lines*. Tehachapi, California. Foothill ridge lines and desert plains are strewn with columns of windmills, taking advantage of the high winds that move west from the San Joaquin Valley to the Mojave Desert. These great turbines generate electricity to meet the insatiable demand of Los Angeles and its suburbs.

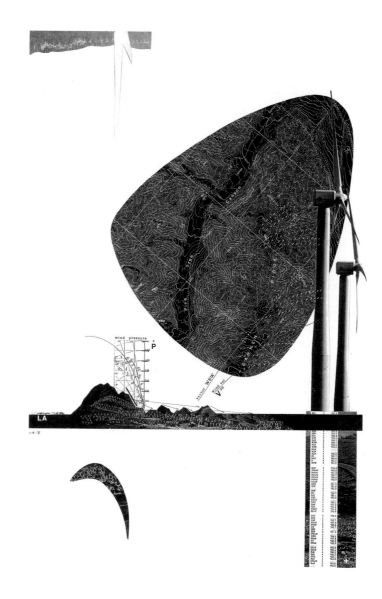

38. *Windmill Topography.* 14 × 20″. The combination of high mountains and desert leads to dramatic contrasts in air temperature and wind pressure. Atmospheric inversions and turbulent airflows are common, resulting in high winds (as well as smog when winds subside). The energy that these airflows yield is captured by strategically sited windmill turbines.

39. *Windmill Row with Roads.* Tehachapi, California.

40. *Windmills.* San Gorgonio Pass, Hot Desert Springs, California. (Photo by James Corner)

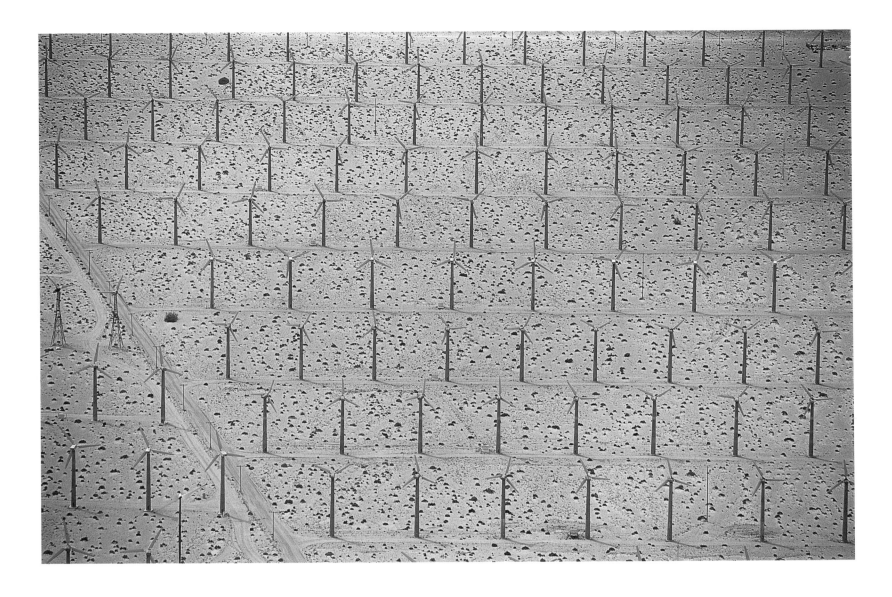

41. *Windmill Field.* Near Palm Springs, California.

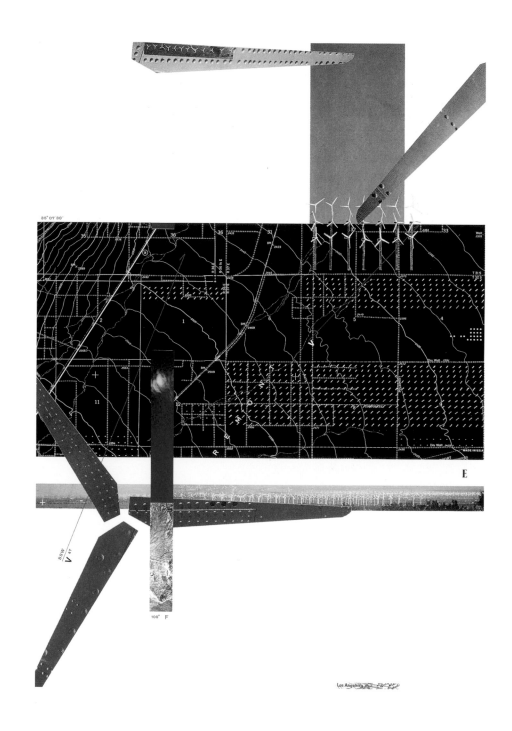

42. *Windmill Fields.* 14 × 20″.

43. *Cluster of Pivot Irrigators.* Tuscarora, Nevada. Long water-sprinkler arms rotate around a central pivot, irrigating circular fields of verdant crops in desert or semiarid environments. Often, a well, located at the center of the circle, pumps water up from vast aquifers in the rock formations below. In Colorado, during 1985, 2.34 billion gallons of groundwater were used daily, primarily for irrigation (a form of excess known as "underground desertification" that cannot be sustained much longer).[4]

44. *Circles of Green.* Farmington, New Mexico.

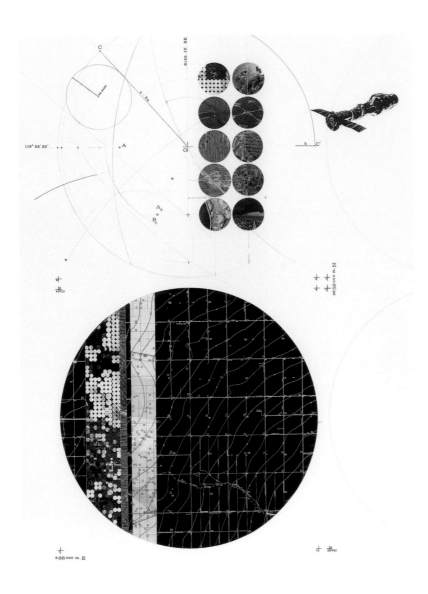

45. *Pivot Irrigators I.* 14 × 20". Sometimes a mile in diameter, these vast circles are constructed using highly specialized survey instruments to make their surfaces level. As the water cools the circular area relative to its surroundings, space satellites sometimes use the resulting infrared temperature patterns as reliable registration marks for orientation.

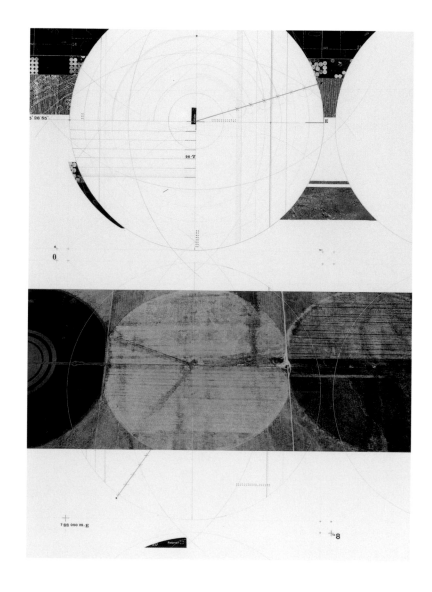

46. *Pivot Irrigators II.* 14 × 20″. The beds of these great circular fields are carefully prepared with underdrainage and irrigation lines. The farmer then divides the area in order to rotate crops and ameliorate soil conditions.[5]

47. *Pivot Irrigator Construction Bed.* San Juan Basin, New Mexico.

48. *Segmented Field.* Teton River, Montana.

49. *Logging Raft alongside Paper Mill.* Bellingham, Washington.

50. *Algae between Logs.* Longview, Washington.

CHAPTER 7

MEASURES OF RULE

A subcategory of the instrumental, measures of rule are those that delineate and coordinate particular sequences of events. In America one finds a number of marks and traces that are testimony to a particular schedule, sequence, or timing of human activity. These are the traces of social life and rhythm upon the land. Lines, elements, patterns, debris, and ruins register the passages of occupancy and labor over time. Weather, season, fallow, rotation, instrument, body, and contingency: all determine the processes by which a people inhabit and measure their ground.

Sometimes, of course, circumstances, needs, and desires change, necessitating the invention and deployment of new rules and markings. At other times, the readjustment of rules precipitates new kinds of activity.

Detail, plate 51.

51. *B-52 "Bone Yards."* Davis-Monthan Air Force Base, Tucson, Arizona. Beginning in the fall of 1993, the United States initiated a three-and-a-half year project to dismember 350 B-52 airplanes to comply with the original Strategic Arms Reduction Treaty. A 13,000-pound guillotine blade dropped from a crane chops the plane into four pieces: nose, midsection, and wings. The remains of each plane are left on the site for 90 days so that Russian satellites can verify the demolition.

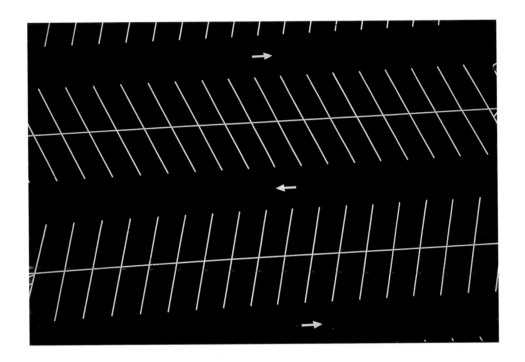

52. *Parking Lot with Stripes*. Taunton, Massachusetts. Markings and delineation upon a surface coordinate activity and spacing.

53. (opposite) *Parking Lot and Tennis Court Overlay*. Annapolis, Maryland. The temporal and programmatic transitions of various activities are often marked on the same surface as a complex overlay.

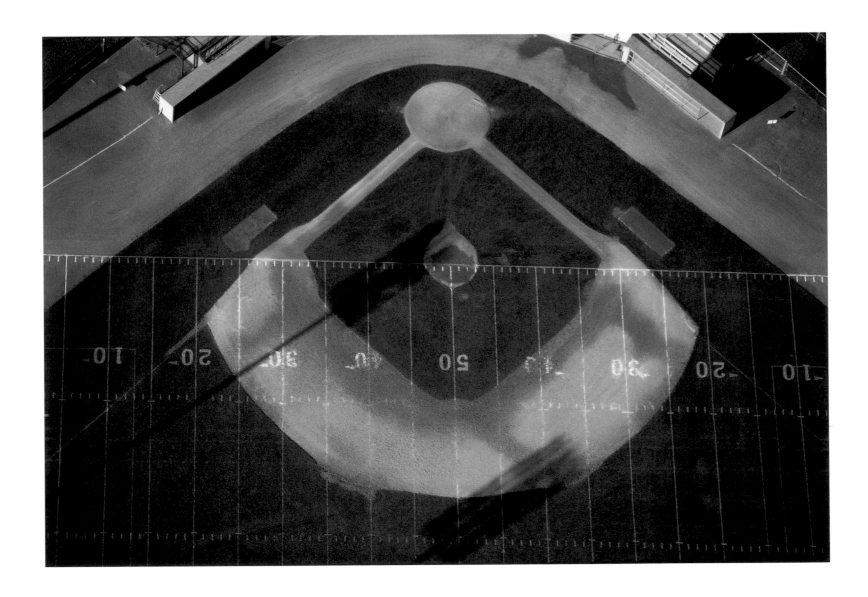

54. *Football Field Edge over Baseball Field.* Minneapolis, Minnesota.

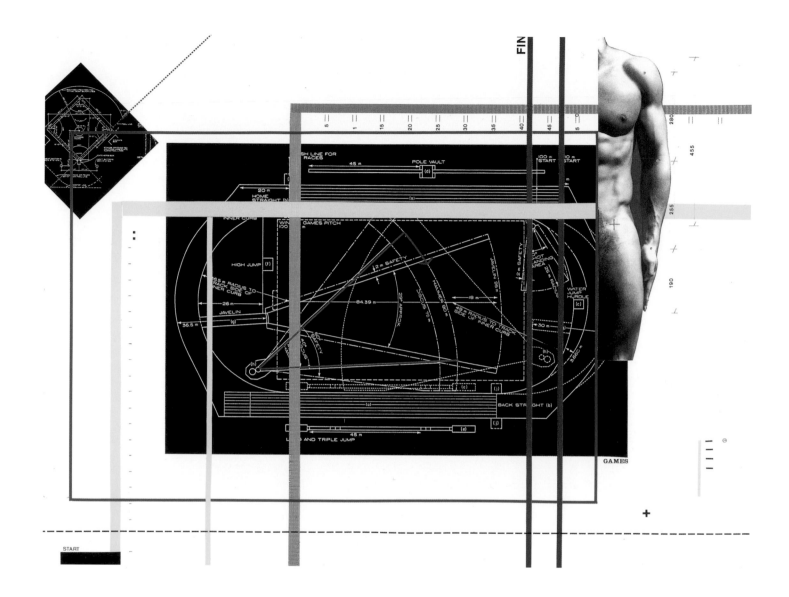

55. *Games.* 12 × 16″. Color-coded upon a surface are different lines of territory, possession, limit, and goal. When the rules change, so too must the game.

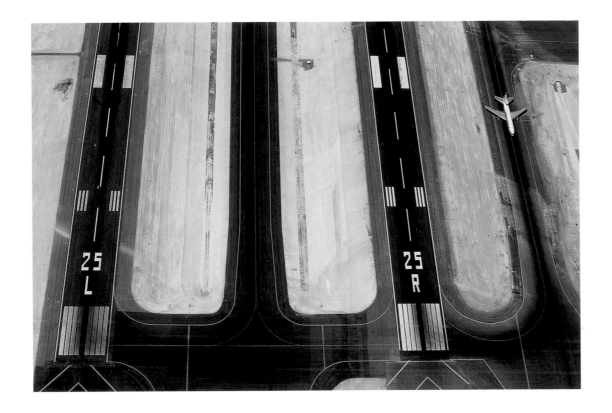

56. *Airport Runway.* Sky Harbor International Airport, Phoenix, Arizona.

57. (opposite) *New Highway Ramps with Construction Markings.* Charlestown, Massachusetts.

58. *A Turning Circle for Trains*. Minneapolis, Minnesota. The railroads enabled the rapid colonization of America during the nineteenth century. Today, the careful routing of rail lines provides an extensive network of communication and transportation across the land, strategically choreographed through schedules, engine allocation, signals, turning circles, sheds, stations, road crossings, and other such measures of coordination.

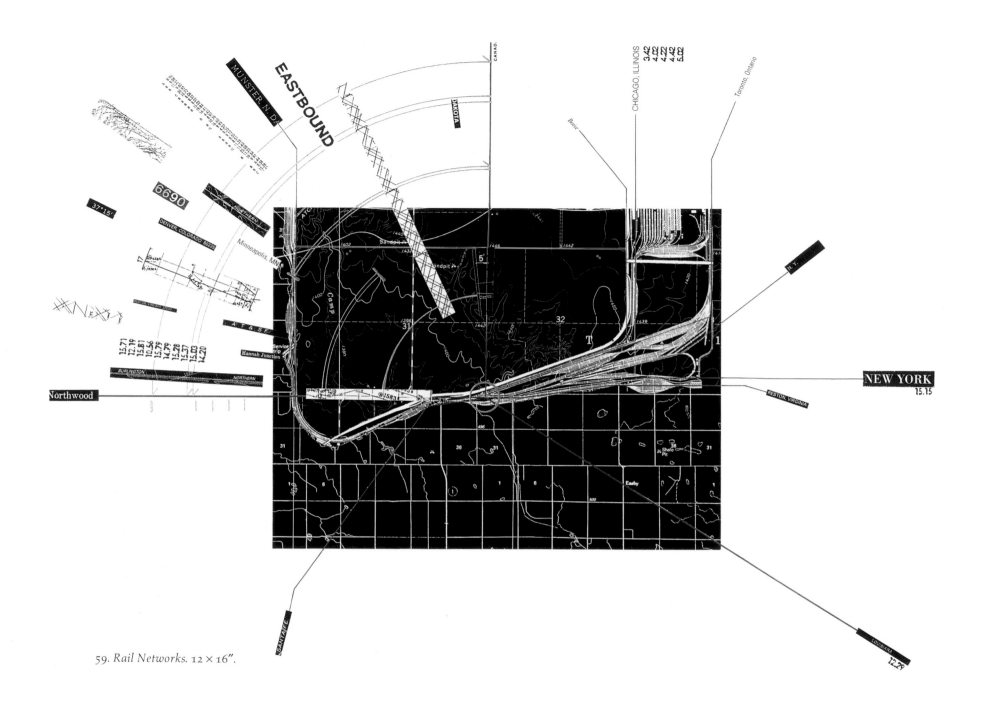

59. *Rail Networks.* 12 × 16".

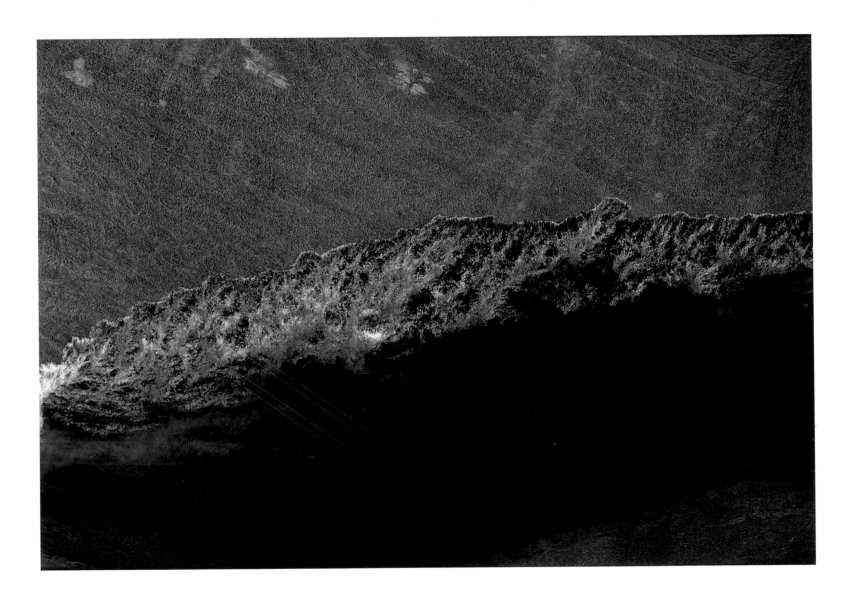

60. *Field Fire.* Columbia area, South Carolina. Fire, though sometimes destructive, can also be a source of renewal in the landscape. When fires are intentionally lit and controlled with regard to winds and temperatures, they can clear fields of old growth and return nutrients to the soil. Without careful control, however, high temperatures can kill essential microorganisms within the soil, rendering it inert and lifeless.

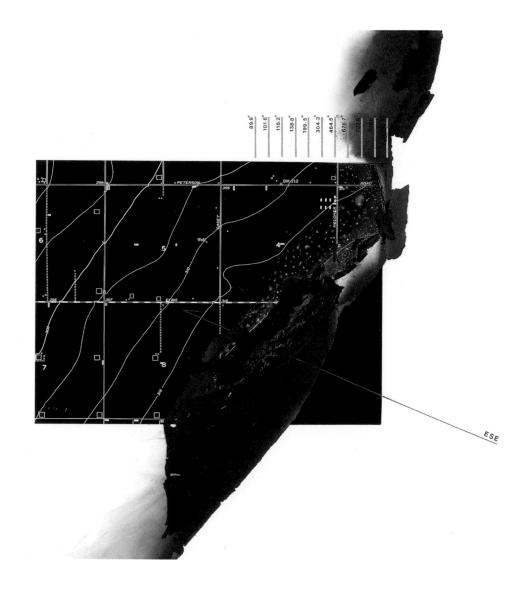

61. Burnings. 12 × 16".

62. *Burning Wheat Furrows.* Snake River Valley, Idaho.

63. *Rice Fields.* Sacramento Valley, California.

64. *Flower Fields.* Oceanside, California.

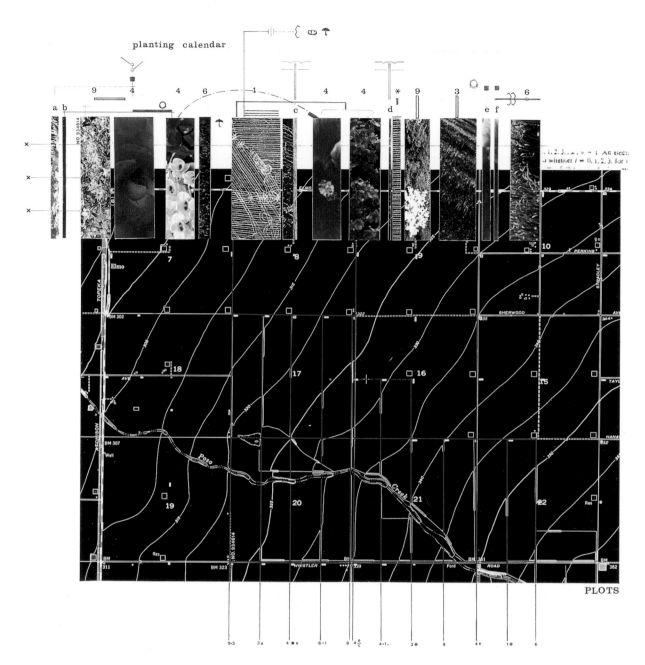

planting calendar

65. *Field Plots.* 12 × 16″. Fields are plotted with great precision. The seeding, sprouting, and blooming times of the various crops involved find expression in the dimensions and rotational schedules of the farmed landscape. The plot is as much about timing and sequence as it is about spacing and marking the ground.

66. *Corn Harvesting.* Eastern Ohio. Fields are never static. Programs of cultivation, growth, harvest, and fallow lend rhythmically changing dimensions to the agricultural landscape.

67. *Amish Field.* Lancaster County, Pennsylvania.

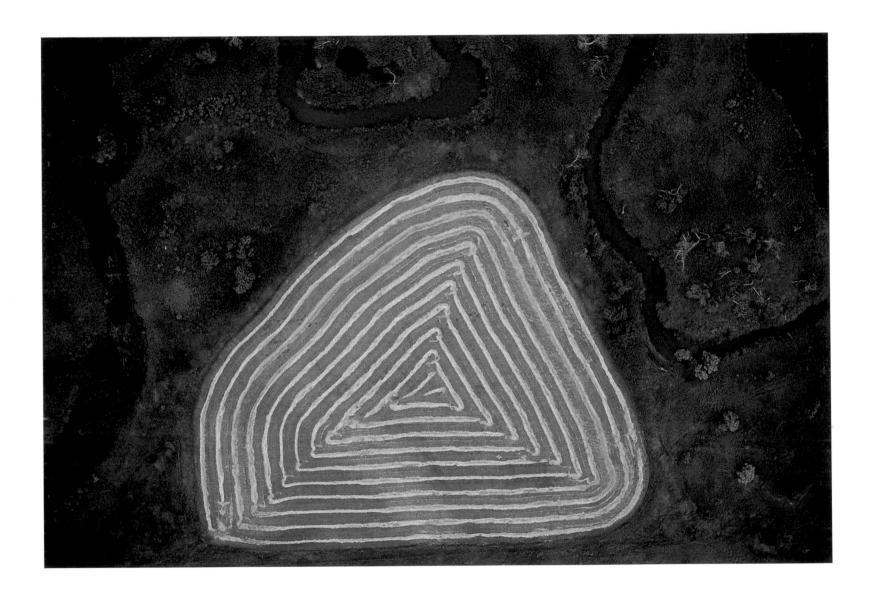

68. *Rings of Hay.* Castleton, North Dakota.

69. *Hay Rings around Old Cemetery.* Westerley, Rhode Island.

70. (opposite) *Field with Grass Strip*. Munich, North Dakota. The landscape of North Dakota is pockmarked with all sorts of depressions, ponds, and hollows, the result of glacial melting twenty thousand years ago. The farmer marks the rules of his occupancy on this uneven surface with grass strips and plowing patterns.

71. *Field with Tractor Lines*. Munich, North Dakota.

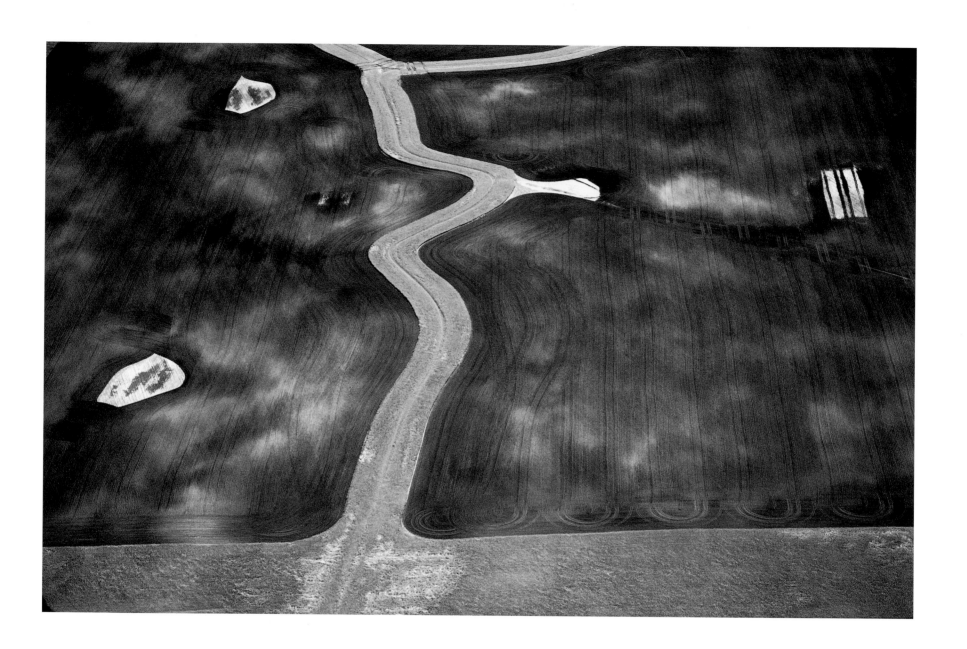

CHAPTER 8

MEASURES OF FIT

The earth is our clock. . . . One, thirty, three hundred and sixty five, those are the units by which our undertakings must be measured.

Le Corbusier

In the landscape, measures of fit structure a beneficial reciprocity between occupant and environment. Through a careful gauging of natural and cultural circumstance, some human communities have adapted their landscapes, buildings, and programs of occupancy to construct a way of life that is in harmony with the ecology of their environment. When things fit, there is no excess or waste, no dominion of one thing over another. Measures that are fitted and fitting, then, unite site, circumstance, and social life with a restrained economy and grace.

Fitting measures are more than template prescriptions, however—cause-and-effect determinism remains an insufficient equation of fittingness. Instead, a fitting measure is one that is also right for a particular circumstance. When things fit, they not only go together physically but are proper for one another in an ethical sense, as if a mutual belonging (or at least a mutual benefit) is being fulfilled. Equitable and reconciliatory, measures of fit precipitate good health and structure well-tempered bonds between things that are different.

Thus, fittingness derives less from calculative accuracy and technical proficiencies than from refined instincts about place and culture, responding always to the play of contingency. Likewise, measured correctness implies not just dimensional exactitude but also social and ethical propriety, bonding the individual into a reciprocal union with others.

Detail, plate 77.

72. *Road Hairpin along Contour.* Tehachapi, California.

73. *Dry-Farming Wheat Strips.* Havre, Montana. Strips of wheat roll across the northern plains of Montana like great carpets laid before the gods. The lonely horizon is punctuated by distant volcanic and geologic features and by the regular spacing of grain elevators and silos along the Burlington Northern Railroad—further measures of admirably negotiated economies. Over the years, farming strategies have also been refined to fit more closely the circumstances of the land.[1]

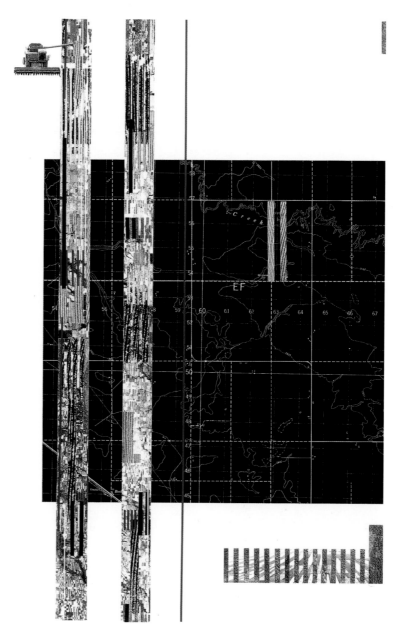

74. *Dry-Farming Strip.* 14 × 20". In the Northern Plains, strips of wheat run north and south, alternating with strips that lie fallow in order to accumulate precious water in these arid, windswept prairies. Sometimes a mile long and only 140 feet wide, the planted strips protect the exposed fallow soil from the drying and erosional effects of strong winds that blow from the west. The ridge and furrow of plow lines mirror this orientation with seed being sown in the protected and damper troughs. The width of each band derives from a carefully gauged degree of effective wind-shelter length for the fallow strips in combination with the dimensions of harvester headers.

75. (opposite) *Dry-Farming Fields with Tractor.* Chester area, Montana.

76. *Field Rolls.* Shelby, Montana.

77. *Wheat Strips on Plateau.* Cutbank, Montana.

78. *Wheat Fields on Tablelands Cut by the Marias River.* Cutbank, Montana.

79. *Wheat Field Contour.* Palouse area, Washington. From the air, field patterns present beautiful and intricate landscapes, yet the true beauty lies within farmers' ability to gauge their strategies of cultivation according to the circumstances of the land. Because soil is their most precious commodity, they must protect exposed areas from erosion caused by rainfall and snowmelt runoff.[2] As a result of plowing, the ridge-and-furrow texture holds water in the troughs and slows surface runoff. Also, crop and fallow rotations in bands between contours allow soil nutrients to be replenished. After harvesting takes place, stubble and stalks are plowed back into the soil and a winter crop is sown as further protection against erosion.

80. *Contour Farming.* 14 × 20″. These striking landscapes of curves, rolls, and turns are literally measured expressions of the farmer's elaborate negotiations with topography, soils, and weather. A dimensional vocabulary accompanies such measures, including phrases such as slope tolerance, pitch, strike, plow depth, plow line, overplow, cross-sow, swale, and datum.

81. *Contour Farming Fields.* McGregor, Iowa.

82. *Contour Fields with Windbreak.* Palouse area, Washington.

83. (opposite) *Wheat Fields*. Palouse area, Washington. The fertile, loessial hills of eastern Washington have a steep, rolling landscape that the wheat farmer must negotiate with care. The light, dusty soils are extremely vulnerable to water and wind erosion, and the steep slopes are difficult for modern farming machinery to work.

84. *Wheat Fields with Burned Areas and Property Line*. Palouse area, Washington. The only straight lines in this sensuous landscape are the fence lines that delineate property, marking the rectilinear overlay of the National Land Survey.

85. *Field Contours.* Lancaster County, Pennsylvania.

86. *Contoured Overplowing.* German Valley, Illinois. Here, the farmer has plowed over the land in a number of ways. First, he plows along the contour to protect from erosion caused by water run-off. Sometime later, using a different plow fixture, he plows back and forth in a straight line perpendicular to the prevailing wind to protect from wind erosion. On both passes, the cultivator is lifted to protect the grass in the low-lying drainage swales.

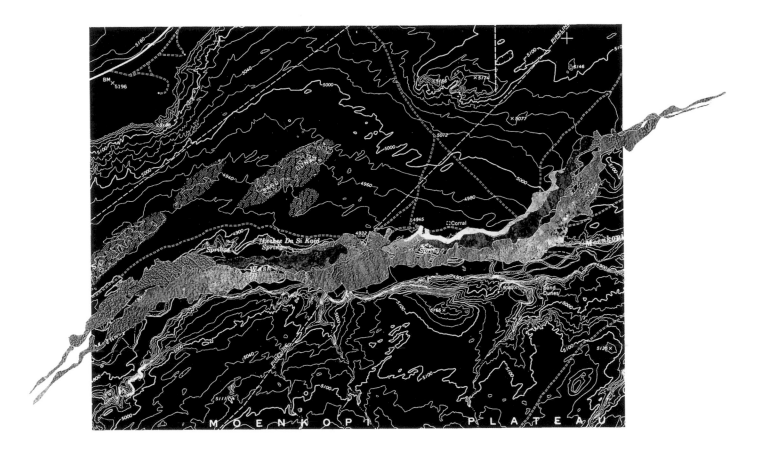

87. (opposite) *Navaho Spring-Line Fields.* Tuba City, Arizona. Seeping slowly out from the bedding plane of a large mesa escarpment in central Arizona is just enough water—if captured and used with care—to grow a verdant garden in the desert. Small, stone check-dams, ditches, and terraces—some built centuries ago by the Anasazi and the Navaho—elaborately conserve and distribute water so that plants and crops can bloom on the sandy washes. Thermal radiation from the cliff walls protects the plants from early frosts.

88. *Navaho Spring-Line Fields.* Tuba City, Arizona. 12 × 16″.

138   Measures of Fit

89. *Shadow across Longhouse Cave.* Mesa Verde, Colorado. Formed by the weathering of spring-lines where permeable sandstone sits over slate, gently arching caves sit in the great cliffs of Mesa Verde. The Anasazi built entire villages in the openings, taking advantage of the natural shelter, its defensibility, the readily available building materials, the flat slate floor, and the spring-line at the back of the cave. Dramatic contrasts between shadow and light move across the cave during the day, creating a wide range of radiant temperatures and serving as eloquent measures of diurnal and seasonal time.

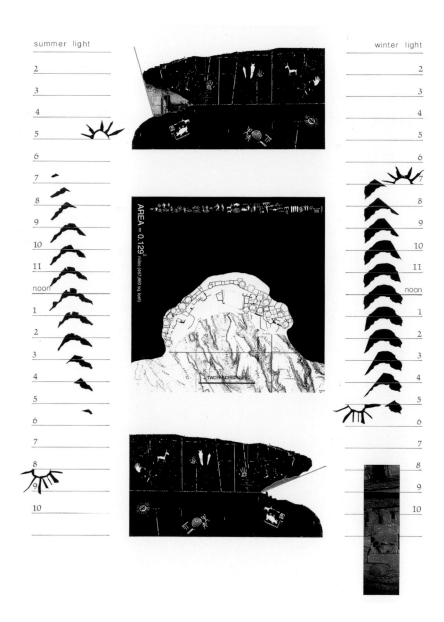

90. *Longhouse Cave.* Mesa Verde, Colorado. 14 × 20". Longhouse is strategically oriented to the south, but the blazing summer sun enters the cave only early in the morning. Large areas of the cave remain in deep shadow for most of the day. In winter, however, the lower altitude and azimuth of the sun allows light to enter the cave immediately at sunrise and to remain there until sunset. The massive sandstone formation absorbs the heat and radiates it slowly during the cold nights. Furthermore, the disposition of buildings within the cave is such that daily activities, like milling corn, cooking, eating, playing, and dancing, move across the cave according to the daily and seasonal movement of temperature, light, and shadow.[3]

91. *Longhouse Cave Dwelling*. Mesa Verde, Colorado. (Photo by James Corner)

> *Far up above me, a thousand feet or so, set in a great cavern in the face of the cliff, I saw a little city of stone asleep. . . . In sunlight it was the color of winter oak leaves. A fringe of cedars grew along the edge of the cavern, like a garden. They were the only living things. Such stillness and repose—immortal repose. . . . I knew at once that I had come upon the city of some extinct civilization, hidden away in this inaccessible mesa for centuries, preserved in the dry air and almost perpetual sunlight like a fly in amber, guarded by the cliffs and the river and the desert.*
>
> Willa Cather

92. (opposite) *Longhouse Cave*. Mesa Verde, Colorado. (Photo by James Corner)

93. *Cave Shadow.* Mesa Verde, Colorado. (Photo by James Corner) The finely gauged measures of each cave's occupancy both instruct and construct the fit of human rhythms with the cycles of nature and the passage of time.

94. *Cave Dwelling and Shadow.* Mesa Verde, Colorado. (Photo by James Corner)

95. *Acoma Pueblo.* Acoma, New Mexico. Parallel rows of houses are carefully sited upon the flat top of a mesa, four hundred feet above the desert plain, in central New Mexico. Planned, gauged, and constructed with economy, the measures of fit at Acoma Pueblo enable its inhabitants to withstand the stresses of living in the desert while demonstrating propriety in the generation of place-form.

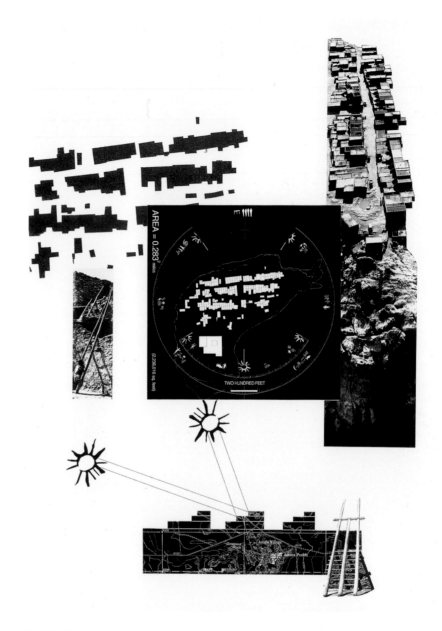

96. *Acoma Pueblo*. Acoma, New Mexico. 14 × 20". The orientation and depth of the houses are such that the dwellings are shaded during the summer but penetrated deeply by light and warmth in winter. Furthermore, the tiered organization exposes a large surface for solar gain in winter, wherein the low angle of winter sunlight is absorbed by thick, heat-retentive clay walls. The three-story-high wall on the northern side is especially thick and has few windows or doors, thereby protecting inhabitants from cold winter winds. During both winter and summer, the third-floor rooms are ablaze in the red light of sunsets. From afar, the city beckons. From within, the thermal radiation of warmth stored in the thick walls helps the family sleep comfortably through the cold desert nights.[4]

CHAPTER 9

MEASURES OF FAITH

Measure-taking is no science. Measure-taking gauges the between which brings the two, heaven and earth, to one another. This measure-taking has its own metron, and thus its own metric.

Martin Heidegger

Measures of faith reconcile the joys and stresses of life with the hopes and revelations of the human spirit. Because the human condition is finite and intimately bound to all other life on the planet, such measures belong to a world that is founded upon the values of hope, respect, and humility. Poetic and fitting, measures of faith belong to a form of awaiting, admitting, and opening that presumes neither closure nor certainty.

Such measures are found in gardens, cemeteries, monuments, and observatories across the American landscape, but they are perhaps most concentrated in the remarkably spiritual landscape of the Southwest. Here, in the vacant luminosity of the arid desert, is a metaphysical emptiness of immeasurable dimension.[1] Expressed throughout this phenomenal and most American of places are occasional gestures by humankind, both ancient and modern, to sound out the void. The dimensions of these constructions are at once modest and grand, manifesting an entire cosmography across myriad scales. Through the poetic precision of these artifacts, the immeasurable is revealed.

Thus, perhaps the ultimate calling of measure in this great land called America is precisely its opposite—the unrepresentable, the wild, and the infinite.

Detail, plate 114.

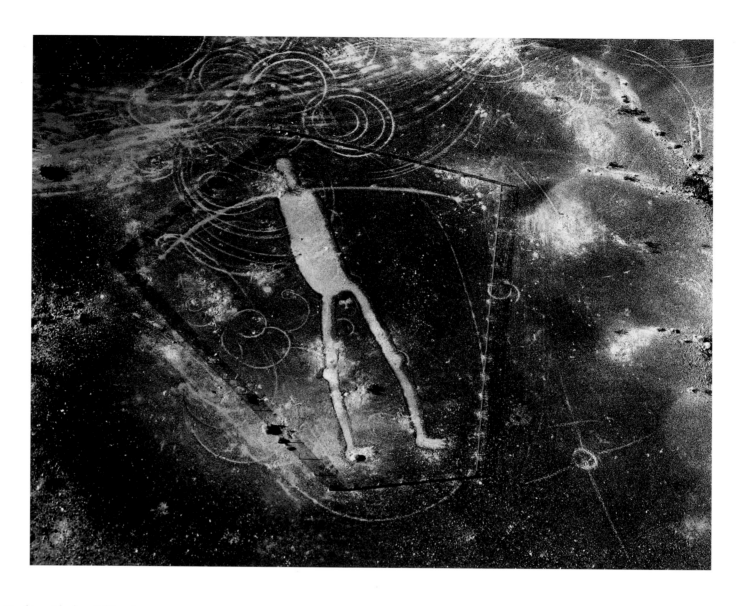

97. *Intaglio Marking.* Blythe, California.

98. *Intaglio Marking.* Blythe, California. Inscribed in the desert floor are figures and symbols of ancient cultures. Made by moving surface material to reveal the lighter sands below, the images are also often surrounded by worn, circular pathways, trails of repeated dances. Perceived kinesthetically and symbolically, these immovable geoglyphs are barely visible from the ground.

99. *Intaglio Figure.* Blythe, California. These great figures remain today as traces that we may never fully understand. The curvilinear ruts made by the four-wheel-drive vehicles of modern day travelers, however, will perhaps endure as a more contemporary overlay of human curiosity and hope.

100. *Cahokia Mounds.* Collinsville, Illinois. Large, geometric earth forms mark out territory on the Mississippi floodplain. Raised tablets of a long-forgotten culture, these mounds once formed the structure of an ancient city engaged in trade, communication, and religious and social ceremonies. The raising of ground had the practical advantage of protecting inhabitants during floods while also giving them a more extensive view across the flat landscape.

101. *Cahokia Mounds along the Mississippi.* Collinsville, Illinois. 14 × 20". The elaborate geometry at Cahokia suggests that the mounds functioned as great symbols of perfection, platforms upon which the most sacred rites would occur and within which the dead were buried and made immortal—measures of permanence across an otherwise undifferentiated, shifting horizon.

102. *Hopi Village and Horizon*. Hopi Indian Reservation, Arizona. For the Hopis, the decision to locate at the very end of the steep mesa promontories that extend out across the expansive flats of the arid desert was both inspired and precarious. In spite of the inhospitable environment, this remote, desolate place is nonetheless the center of the Hopi universe.

 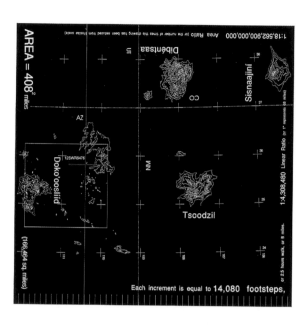 

103. *Hopi Cosmography.* 14 × 20″.

The man of the archaic societies tends to live as much as possible in the sacred or in close proximity to consecrated objects. The tendency is perfectly understandable, because, for primitives as for the man of all pre-modern societies, the sacred is equivalent to a power, and in the last analysis, to reality.

Mircea Eliade

Surrounded and watched over by the four sacred mountains (to the east, west, north, and south) and oriented by a striking horizon of distant cones and clefts, the Hopi believe themselves to be duly positioned to receive favorable treatment from the gods.[2]

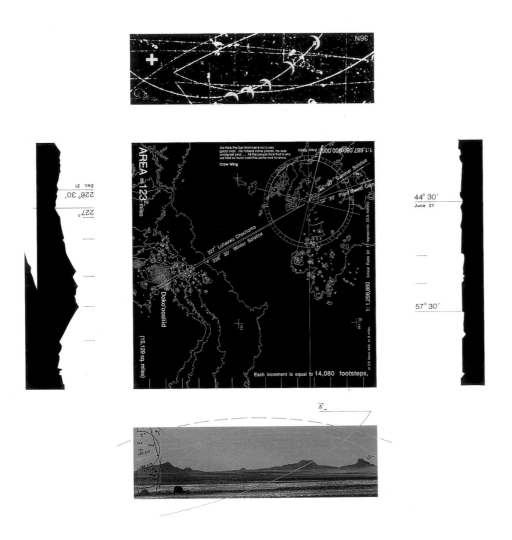

104. *Hopi Horizon Calendar.* 14 × 20".

And the heraldry of the horizon must have encouraged him to suspect that if he stood fast the Gods might help him there.

Vincent Scully

Hopi time is constructed by the track of the sun across the dramatically marked horizon. As the sun rises and sets in a more extreme location along the horizon each day, and turns back at times of solstice, the Hopi use the geological calibrations across the distant landscape as a timepiece, a calendar to predict times for planting, harvest, and religious ceremony. The solstices are the most important times of observation for the Hopi, as the sun's movement slows and rests for a few days prior to returning along the horizon and bringing in the new season. If the sun were to stay too long at its "winter house," a long, cold winter followed by spring frosts might delay planting and damage young crops; whereas if it failed to stay long enough in its "summer house," the growing season might be too short for a good harvest.[3] Measured with anticipation and hope, the track of the sun along the horizon constructs the varying rhythms of being in time.

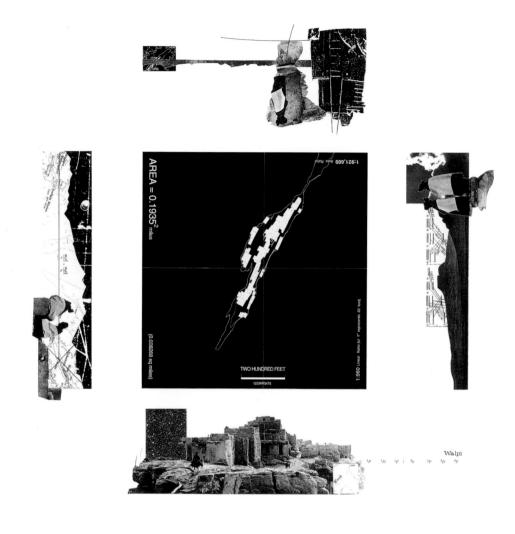

105. *Hopi Village of Walpi.* 14 × 20".

Let us no longer say that time is a datum of consciousness; let us be more precise and say that consciousness deploys or constitutes time.

Maurice Merleau-Ponty

106. *Walpi*. Hopi Indian Reservation, Arizona. Like the navigation and communication rooms stacked on the decks of great ships, the Hopi villages probe the expansive sea of the desert below and the sky above for clues regarding changes in weather, season, and fortune. Sited on elongated fingers of rock, the three main villages have a constructed unity through lines of sight and communication. The main public space of Walpi is situated along the eastern flank, marked by the sacred Snake Rock, a residual column of stone. Underground Kivas, or religious rooms, line the edge of the space and are punctured with small apertures that register features along the horizon and in the adjacent village. The entrances to these secret planning and speculation chambers are marked with the long, spindly poles of ladders that reach upward to the sky.[4] The entire Hopi cosmography is constructed, with restraint, to capture the sacred reality of the landscape and its occupation.

107. *Pueblo Bonito.* Chaco Canyon, New Mexico. Astronomically and geographically aligned, the highly ordered complex of Pueblo Bonito sits at the center of the ancient Chacoan world. Embodied in the pueblo's layout and construction, and perceived in its cool, amberlike rooms, is an entire cosmography revealed through light. Walls, pathways, window openings, and lines of communication across the landscape are each measured with precision so as to reveal the rhythmical patterns of the cosmos. The circular rooms are called Kivas. These places for spiritual and religious life are entirely enclosed and sunk into the earth.[5]

108. *Pueblo Bonito.* Chaco Canyon, New Mexico. 14 × 20".

In the homogeneous and infinite expanse, in which no point of reference is possible and hence no orientation can be established, the hierophany reveals an absolute fixed point, a center. . . . It is for this reason that religious man has always sought to fix his abode at "the center of the world."

Mircea Eliade

109. *Window at Pueblo Bonito*. Chaco Canyon, New Mexico. (Photo by James Corner) Carefully placed window openings in the delicately constructed stone walls at Bonito mark particular formations in the sky while allowing light into rooms. At special times of year, the correspondence of solar angles with certain window apertures casts pools of light onto walls and floors in specific geometric shapes and figures, effectively binding human routine into the life of a greater cosmos.[6]

110. *Interior Room with Doorway at Pueblo Bonito.* (Photo by James Corner) Within the cool, silent rooms of Bonito, there is a rarefied atmosphere, a mazelike and richly detailed complexity that contrasts sharply with the bright, vast emptiness of the landscape.

111. *Fajada Butte.* Chaco Canyon, New Mexico. An isolated butte stands majestically upon the washes and arroyos of Chaco Canyon, providing a significant marker on the near horizon for the Chacoan people.

112. *Fajada Butte Shadow.* Chaco Canyon, New Mexico. Light and shadow, sun and moon: the most elemental cycles that construct our human rhythms and symbolic worlds are measured with eloquent precision in an elaborate but modest astronomical assembly on one side of the butte.

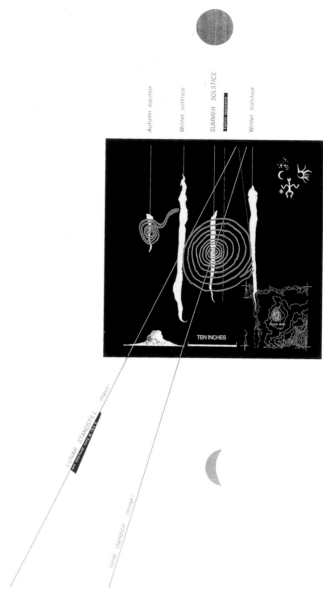

113. *Spiral Calendar at Fajada Butte.* Chaco Canyon, New Mexico. 14 × 20″. Close to the summit of Fajada Butte, on a vertical cliff, an arrangement of large stones shields two spirals, one large and one small, drawn into the rock wall. With remarkable precision, the morning sun on the day of summer solstice draws a "dagger" of bright light through the center of the larger spiral. At winter solstice, two daggers of light exactly frame the outer edges of the spiral. Times of equinox are also recorded. Moreover, at times of lunar standstill a dark shadow bisects the spiral. There are also ten turns of the spiral on the left of center and nine on the right, paralleling the alternation of ten- and nine-year ecliptic cycles. The total of nineteen turns parallels the lunar declination cycle, which is slightly less than nineteen years. Shrine and observatory, the calendrical spiral at Fajada Butte both measures and embodies the unity of natural and human time.[7]

114. *Horizon Marked by Very Large Array Radio Telescope.* Magdalena, New Mexico. (Photo by James Corner) Sited on the high mountain plains of St. Agustin, Magdalena, is the Very Large Array Radio Telescope (V.L.A.). The installation takes advantage of a stable geology and a high-altitude plain that is remote from the interference of cities. These radio-telescope dishes point upward to the universe, listening patiently to the murmurs of its depths. Reminiscent of more ancient observatories, these dishes mark the horizon at precise intervals.

115. *V.L.A. Dishes and Track*. Magdalena, New Mexico. (Photo by James Corner) Spaced along three rail tracks, each fifteen miles long and radiating in a Y-shape from a single center, are twenty-seven dishes, each an eighty-two-foot antenna. Collectively, these dishes function as a single, large receiver equivalent to twenty-one miles in diameter. The dishes can be moved along the tracks and rearranged in order to pinpoint their focus of attention in deep space.[8]

116. *V.L.A. Dish at End of Track.* Magdalena, New Mexico. In this vast, empty landscape is a spacing that listens with patient restraint, without assertion or domination; a spacing that remains open to any number of other configurations so as to listen more clearly; and a spacing that ultimately embodies a sense of cosmic order and hope.

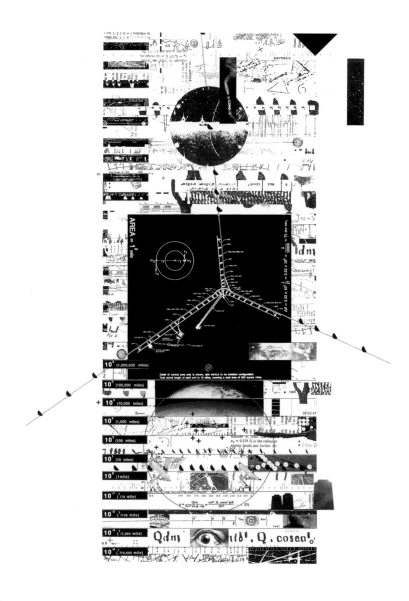

117. *V.L.A. : Powers of Ten I.* 14 × 20″. As in ancient times, the angels of the heavens are revealed as constructed angles upon the ground, measured in the alternative spacing of these beacons along the horizon. In this still landscape, the micro-exactitude of modern instruments increasingly encompasses the full magnitude of the galaxies: nano-microns on earth become scaled-down mirror measures of light years across space.[9]

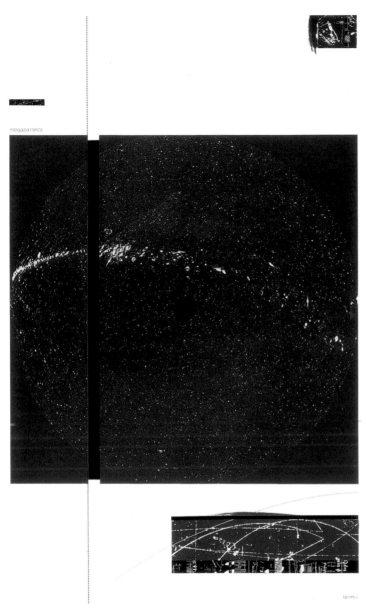

megaparsecs

fermis

118. *V.L.A.: Measures of Silence.* 14 × 20". The central image is a survey scan of the northern sky at 1,400 MHz. The map is centered on the celestial pole and reaches 5 degrees below the celestial equator at the circumference. The curved band traces the plane of the galaxy, wherein several supernova remnants can be seen. The huge numbers of small stars scattered across the sky are actually luminous radio sources in extremely distant elliptical galaxies and quasars.[10] The lower black image is of charged Sigma and K particles, produced when a pion hits a proton in a bubble chamber.

119. *V.L.A.: X.* 14 × 20".

> *For the listener, who listens in the snow,*
> *And, nothing himself, beholds*
> *Nothing that is not there and the nothing that is.*

Wallace Stevens

NOTES

Preface

1. One of the most thorough and influential works on aerial photography is E. A. Gutkind's *Our World from the Air: An International Survey of Man and His Environment* (Garden City, N.Y.: Doubleday, 1952). Of particular analytical merit with regard to the American landscape is Francis Joseph Marshner, *Land Use and Its Patterns in the United States*, Agriculture Handbook no. 153 (Washington, D.C.: U.S. Department of Agriculture, 1959). There are numerous books that artistically depict the surface of the earth from the air, most notably, Marilyn Bridges, *Markings: Aerial Views of Sacred Landscapes* (New York: Aperture/SADEV, 1986); William Garnett, *The Extraordinary Landscape: Aerial Photographs of America* (Boston: Little, Brown, 1982); Georg Gerster, *Amber Waves of Grain: America's Farmlands from Above* (New York: Harper, Weldon, Owen, 1990); Georg Gerster, *Below from Above* (New York: Abbeville, 1986); Georg Gerster, *Grand Design: The Earth from Above* (New York: Paddington, 1976); Emmett Gowin, *Photographs* (Philadelphia: Philadelphia Museum of Art, 1990); Alex MacLean and Bill McKibben, *Look at the Land: Aerial Reflections on America* (New York: Rizzoli, 1993); Hanns Reich, *The World from Above* (New York: Hill and Wang, 1966).

Detail, plate 58.

Introduction

1. For superb descriptions of Alex MacLean's flying practices, see MacLean and McKibben, *Look at the Land*; and Donna Gordon, "Flight Patterns," *Boston Globe Magazine*, July 24, 1994, 10–33.

2. This faith, or indulgence, in happenstance was not without some risk, however. Owing to a particularly odd turn of events, we nearly lost our lives one night during a landing in the fields of Maryland. Although the plane was a total wreck, we escaped without a scratch.

3. Roland Barthes, *Camera Lucida*, translated by Richard Howard (New York: Hill and Wang, 1981).

4. On the imaginative effects of photographs upon the subsequent apprehension of reality, see Paul Vanderbilt, *Between the Landscape and Its Other* (Baltimore: Johns Hopkins University Press, 1993); Victor Burgin, ed., *Thinking Photography* (London: Macmillan, 1982); Estelle Jussim and Elizabeth Lindquist–Cock, *Landscape as Photograph* (New Haven: Yale University Press, 1985).

5. Morris M. Thompson, *Maps for America: Cartographic Products of the U.S. Geological Survey and Others*, 2d ed. (Washington, D.C.: U.S. Department of the Interior, 1981).

6. Denis Cosgrove, *The Palladian Landscape: Geographical Change and Its Cultural Representations in Sixteenth-Century Italy* (State College: Pennsylvania State University Press, 1993); Alberto Perez-Gomez, *Architecture and the Crisis of Modern Science* (Cambridge: MIT Press, 1983).

7. On the shift from traditional to modern uses of measure, see Witold Kula, *Measures and Men*, translated by R. Szreter (Princeton: Princeton University Press, 1986).

Chapter 1:
The Measures of America

1. Stephen Kern, *The Culture of Time and Space, 1880–1918* (Cambridge: Harvard University Press, 1983); David Harvey, *The Condition of Postmodernity: An Enquiry into the Origins of Cultural Change* (Oxford: Basil Blackwell, 1989).

2. Dean McCannell, *Empty Meeting Grounds: The Tourist Papers* (London: Routledge, 1992).

3. E. A. Gutkind, "Our World from the Air: Conflict and Adaptation," in *Man's Role in Changing the Face of the Earth*, edited by W. L. Thomas (Chicago: Chicago University Press, 1956), 1.

4. Denis Cosgrove, "Contested Global Visions: One-World, Whole-Earth, and the Apollo Space Photographs," *Annals of the Association of American Geographers* 84, no. 2 (1994): 270–94; Alexander Wilson, *The Culture of Nature: North American Landscape from Disney to the Exxon Valdez* (Oxford: Basil Blackwell, 1992).

5. Alfred W. Crosby, *The Columbian Exchange: Biological and Cultural Consequences of 1492* (Westport, Conn.: Greenwood, 1972).

6. Cosgrove, *The Palladian Landscape.*

7. William Q. Boelhower, *Through a Glass Darkly: Ethnic Semiosis in American Literature* (Venice: Helvetia, 1984), 50–51.

8. William M. Denevan, "The Pristine Myth: The Landscape of the Americas in 1492," *Annals of the Association of American Geographers* 82, no. 3 (1992): 369–87.

9. Peter Hulme, *Colonial Encounters: Europe and the Native Caribbean, 1492–1797* (London: Routledge, 1986).

10. Robert Lawson-Peebles, *Landscape and Written Expression in Revolutionary America* (Cambridge: Cambridge University Press, 1988).

11. Archibald MacLeish, "America Was Promises," in *New and Collected Poems, 1917–76* (Boston: Houghton Mifflin, 1976), 328.

12. Kern, *The Culture of Time and Space.*

13. Donald Worster, *Rivers of Empire: Water, Aridity, and the Growth of the American West* (New York: Pantheon, 1985).

14. Donald Worster, *Dust Bowl: The Southern Plains in the 1930s* (New York: Oxford University Press, 1979).

15. David Matless, "A Modern Stream: Water, Landscape, Modernism, and Geography," *Environment and Planning D: Society and Space* 10 (1992): 569–88.

16. Richard Misrach, *Bravo 20: The Bombing of the American West* (Baltimore: Johns Hopkins University Press, 1990).

17. James E. Vance, "California and the Search for the Ideal," *Annals of the Association of American Geographers* 62 (1972): 185–220.

18. Quoted in Agnes Heller, *Renaissance Man*, translated by Richard E. Allen (Boston: Routledge and Kegan Paul, 1978), 451.

Chapter 2:
Aerial Representation and the Making of Landscape

1. Le Corbusier, *Aircraft: The New Vision* (1935; reprint, New York: Universe, 1988), 5, 96.

2. Ian McHarg, *Design with Nature*, 2d ed. (New York: Wiley, 1992).

3. James Duncan and David Ley, eds., *Place/Culture/Representation* (London: Routledge, 1993); Denis Cosgrove and Stephen Daniels, eds., *The Iconography of Landscape* (Cambridge: Cambridge University Press, 1988); Svetlana Alpers, *The Art of Describing: Dutch Art in the Seventeenth Century* (Chicago: University of Chicago Press, 1983); D. W. Meinig, "The Beholding Eye," *The Interpretation of Ordinary Landscapes*, edited by D. W. Meinig (New York: Oxford University Press, 1979), 33–48.

4. E. H. Gombrich, *Art and Illusion: A Study in the Psychology of Pictorial Representation* (Princeton: Princeton University Press, 1961); Jonathan Crary, *Techniques of the Observer: On Vision and Modernity in the Nineteenth Century* (Cambridge: MIT Press, 1990); Kenneth Clark, *Landscape into Art* (New York: Harper and Row, 1976); Hans-Georg Gadamer, *Truth and Method*, 2d rev. ed., translated by J. Weinsheimer and D. G. Marshall (New York: Crossroads, 1990).

5. J. B. Harley, "Maps, Knowledge, and Power," in *The Iconography of Landscape*, 277–312; Trevor J. Barnes and James Duncan, eds., *Writing Worlds: Discourse, Text, and Metaphor in the Representation of Landscape* (London: Routledge, 1992).

6. Denis Wood, *The Power of Maps* (London: Guilford Press, 1992).

7. John Pickles, "Text, Hermeneutics, and Propaganda Maps," in *Writing Worlds*, 193–230; W. J. T. Mitchell, ed., *Landscape and Power* (Chicago: University of Chicago Press, 1994).

8. For a remarkable example of satellite images conjoined with maps and environmental inventories, see National Geographic Society, *Atlas of North America: Space-Age Portrait of a Continent* (Washington, D.C.: National Geographic Society, 1985).

9. Richard Long, *Walking in Circles* (London: South Bank Center, 1991); Rudolf Herman Fuchs, *Richard Long* (London: Thames and Hudson; New York: Solomon R. Guggenheim Museum, 1986).

Chapter 3: The American
Landscape at Work

1. John Brinkerhoff Jackson, *A Sense of Place, a Sense of Time* (New Haven: Yale University Press, 1994); Leo Marx, *The Machine in the Garden: Technology and the Pastoral Idea in America* (New York: Oxford University Press, 1964); Reyner Banham, *Scenes in America Deserta* (Salt Lake City: Peregrine Smith, 1982); Barbara Stouffacher Solomon, *Good Mourning California* (New York: Rizzoli, 1992).

2. Daniel Boorstein, *The Americans: The Democratic Experience* (New York: Vintage, 1974); Stephen Kurtz, *Wasteland: Building the American Dream* (New York: Praeger, 1973); Ellis Armstrong, ed., *History of Public Works in the United States, 1776–1976* (Chicago: American Public Works Association, 1976);

Jean Baudrillard, *America*, translated by Chris Turner (London: Verso, 1988).

3. Baudrillard, "Utopia Achieved," in *America*, 75–105.

Chapter 4: Taking Measure

1. For more elaborate, philosophical descriptions of this situation, see Gianni Vattimo, *The End of Modernity*, translated by Jon Snyder (Baltimore: Johns Hopkins University Press, 1991); Gianni Vattimo, *The Transparent Society*, translated by David Webb (Baltimore: Johns Hopkins University Press, 1992).

2. Baudrillard, *America*, 28.

3. Alexis de Tocqueville, *Democracy in America*, translated by George Lawrence, edited by J. P. Mayer and Max Lerner (New York: Harper and Row, 1966); Claude Lefort, *Democracy and Political Theory*, translated by David Macey (Minneapolis: University of Minnesota Press, 1988).

4. See, e.g., Hans-Georg Gadamer, *The Relevance of the Beautiful and Other Essays*, translated by Nicolas Water and edited by Robert Bernasconi (Cambridge: Cambridge University Press, 1986).

5. Kula, *Measures and Men*, 29–30.

6. Ibid., 120.

7. Ibid., 121; Adrien Favre, *Les origines du système métrique* (Paris: Presses Universitaires de France, 1931).

8. Edwin Morris Betts, ed., *Thomas Jefferson's Garden Book, 1766–1824* (Philadelphia: American Philosophical Society, 1944), 4–5.

9. Thomas Jefferson, *Notes on the State of Virginia* (1785); quoted in Ralph E. Griswold and Frederick D. Nichols, *Thomas Jefferson*

Landscape Architect (Charlottesville: University of Virginia Press, 1978), 4.

10. Quoted in Hildegard Binder Johnson, *Order upon the Land: The U.S. Rectangular Survey and the Upper Mississippi County* (New York: Oxford University Press, 1976), 39.

11. Ibid., 40–49.

12. Ibid., 77.

13. John Fraser Hart, *The Look of the Land* (Englewood Cliffs, N.J.: Prentice-Hall, 1975), 48–49; John Francis McDermott, *The French in the Mississippi Valley* (Urbana: University of Illinois Press, 1965).

14. David Leatherbarrow, "Qualitative Proportions and Elastic Geometry," in *The Roots of Architectural Invention: Site, Enclosure, Materials* (Cambridge: Cambridge University Press, 1993), 107–19.

15. Jacques Derrida, "Point de folie—maintenant l'architecture," in *La case vide: La villette*, Bernard Tschumi (London: Architectural Association, 1986), 7.

16. Martin Heidegger, ". . . Poetically Man Dwells . . . , " in *Poetry, Language, Thought*, translated by Albert Hofstadter (New York: Harper and Row, 1971), 221.

17. Ibid., 221.

18. Ibid., 228.

19. Albert Hofstadter, *Agony and Epitaph: Man, His Art, and His Poetry* (New York: George Braziller, 1970), 2.

20. Karston Harries, "The Many Uses of Metaphor," in *On Metaphor*, edited by Sheldon Sacks (Chicago: University of Chicago Press, 1978), 165–72.

21. Hofstadter, *Agony and Epitaph*, 1–5; Werner Marx, *Is There a Measure on Earth?* translated by Thomas J. Nenon and Reginald Lilly (Chicago: University of Chicago Press, 1987).

22. Ibid., 254.

23. See Marc Reisner, *Cadillac Desert* (New York: Viking Penguin, 1986); Philip L. Fradkin, *A River No More: The Colorado River and the West* (Tucson: University of Arizona Press, 1984); Worster, *Rivers of Empire*. In discussing the hydroengineering projects along the Colorado River, Reisner recognizes the paradox of these measures, referring to them as "a uniquely productive, creative vandalism" (503).

24. Vattimo, "Utopia, Counter-utopia, Irony," in *The Transparent Society*, 76–88.

25. Johnson, *Order upon the Land*, 239–42; Michael Conzen, ed., *The Making of the American Landscape* (London: Harper and Collins, 1990).

26. Interestingly perhaps, these last phrases echo those of the surrealists (like André Breton or Max Ernst), who were struggling, in their own way, with the increasing objectification of the world and the primacy of the rational over other modes of thought and action. See also, Kevin Kelly, *Out of Control: The New Biology of Machines, Social Systems, and the Economic World* (Reading, Mass.: Addison-Wesley, 1994).

Chapter 5: Measures of Land

1. John Stilgoe, *Common Landscape of America, 1580 to 1845* (New Haven: Yale University Press, 1982), 14–15, 50–51; John Brinkerhoff Jackson, "The Westward-Moving House," in *Landscapes: Selected Writings of J. B. Jackson*, edited by Ervin H. Zube (Amherst: University of Massachusetts Press, 1970), 10–42; Scott R. Sanders, *Wilderness*

Plots (New York: William Morrow, 1983).

2. Johnson, *Order upon the Land*, 64–72.

3. Ibid., 53–82; Stilgoe, *Common Landscape of America*, 99–107; Lowell Stewart, *Public Land Surveys* (New York: Arno Press, 1979); Wallace Stegner, *Beyond the Hundredth Meridian: John Wesley Powell and the Second Opening of the West* (Boston: Houghton Mifflin, 1954).

4. Johnson, *Order upon the Land*, 57–8.

5. McDermott, *The French in the Mississippi Valley*.

Chapter 6: Measures of Control

1. John McPhee, *The Control of Nature* (New York: Noonday Press/Farrar, Straus and Giroux, 1989); Worster, *Rivers of Empire*; Armstrong, *History of Public Works in the United States*; Conzen, *The Making of the American Landscape*.

2. Jacques Ellul, *The Technological Society*, translated by John Wilkinson (New York: Knopf, 1964); Marx, *The Machine in the Garden*.

3. Reisner, *Cadillac Desert*; Fradkin, *A River No More*; Worster, *Rivers of Empire*; Norris Hundley, *Water and West: The Colorado River Compact and the Politics of Water in the American West* (Berkeley: University of California Press, 1975).

4. Reisner, *Cadillac Desert*, 452–94; Kenneth Helphand, *Colorado: Visions of an American Landscape* (Niwot, Colo.: Roberts Rinehart, 1991), 130.

5. William E. Splinter, "Center-Pivot Irrigation," *Scientific American* 234, no. 6 (1976).

Chapter 8: Measures of Fit

Epigraphs: (p. 121) Le Corbusier, *The Radiant City* (New York: Orion, 1964), 77; (p. 142) Willa Cather, *The Professor's House* (New York: Alfred Knopf, 1925), 201–02.

1. Mary W. Hargreaves, *Dry Farming in the Northern Great Plains, 1900–1925* (Cambridge: Harvard University Press, 1957).

2. U.S. Department of Agriculture, *Contours of Change* (Washington, D.C.: U.S.D.A., 1970); Gerster, *Amber Waves of Grain*; Marshner, *Land Use and Its Patterns in the United States*.

3. Ralph Knowles, *Energy and Form: An Ecological Approach to Urban Form* (Cambridge: MIT Press, 1974), 20–26.

4. Knowles, *Energy and Form*, 27–33; J. W. Fewkes, "The Sun's Influence on the Form of Hopi Pueblos," *American Anthropologist* 8 (1906): 88–100; Stanley Stubbs, *A Bird's-Eye View of the Pueblos* (Norman: University of Oklahoma Press, 1950).

Chapter 9: Measures of Faith

Epigraphs: (p. 149) Heidegger, *Poetry, Language, Thought*, 221; (p. 157) Mircea Eliade, *The Sacred and the Profane: The Nature of Religion*, translated by W. R. Trask (New York: Harcourt, Brace, Jovanovich, 1959), 12; (p. 158) Vincent Scully, *Pueblo: Mountain, Village, Dance*, 2d ed. (Chicago: University of Chicago Press, 1989), 303; (p. 159) Maurice Merleau-Ponty, *Phenomenology of Perception*, translated by Colin Smith (London: Routledge and Kegan Paul, 1962), 412; (p. 162) Eliade, *Sacred and the Profane*, 21–22; (p. 173) Wallace Stevens, "Snow Man," in *Collected Poems* (New York: Knopf, 1981), 10.

1. Mark C. Taylor, "Desertion," in *Disfiguring: Art, Architecture, Religion* (Chicago: University of Chicago Press, 1992), 269–307; Banham, *Scenes in America Deserta*; Baudrillard, "Desert for Ever," in *America*, 121–28.

2. Frank Waters, *The Book of the Hopi* (New York: Viking Press, 1963); Barton Wright, *Pueblo Cultures* (Leiden: E. J. Brill, 1986); Laura Gilpin, *The Enduring Navajo* (Austin: University of Texas Press, 1968).

3. Leo William Simmons, ed., *Sun Chief: The Autobiography of a Hopi Indian* (New Haven: Yale University Press, 1972), 57–60; J. McKim Malville and Claudia Putnam, *Prehistoric Astronomy in the Southwest* (Boulder, Colo.: Johnson, 1991), 16–19; Michael Zeilik, "Keeping the Sacred and Planting Calendar: Archaeoastronomy in the Pueblo Southwest," in *World Archaeoastronomy*, edited by Anthony F. Aveni (Cambridge: Cambridge University Press, 1989), 143–166.

4. Scully, *Pueblo*, 317–49.

5. David Grant Noble, ed., *New Light on Chaco Canyon* (Santa Fe: School of American Research Press, 1984); Neil M. Judd, *The Architecture of Pueblo Bonito*, Smithsonian Miscellaneous Collections, vol. 147, no. 1 (Washington, D.C.: Smithsonian Institution, 1964); Kendrick Frazier, *People of Chaco: A Canyon and Its Culture* (New York: Norton, 1986).

6. Michael Zeilik, "Keeping a Seasonal Calendar at Pueblo Bonito," *Archaeoastronomy* 9 (1986): 79–87; J. E. Reyman, "Astronomy, Architecture, and Adaptation at Pueblo Bonito," *Science* 193 (1976): 957–62.

7. A. Sofaer, A. V. Zinser, and R. M. Sinclair. "A Unique Solar Marking Construct," *Science* 206 (1979): 283–91; and A. Sofaer, R. M. Sinclair,

and L. E. Doggett. "Lunar Markings on Fajada Butte, Chaco Canyon, New Mexico," in *Archaeoastronomy in the New World,* edited by Anthony F. Aveni (Cambridge: Cambridge University Press, 1982), 169–81; Malville and Putnam, *Prehistoric Astronomy,* 30–33.

8. National Radio Astronomy Observatory, *The Very Large Array* (Socorro, N.M.: NRAO/AUI, 1989); D. S. Heeschen, "The Very Large Array," in *Telescopes for the 1980s,* edited by G. Burbridge and A. Hewitt (Palo Alto: Annual Reviews, 1981), 1–61; A. Richard Thompson, James Moran, and George W. Swensen, *Interferometry and Synthesis in Radio Astronomy* (New York: Wiley, 1986); Lys Ann Shore, "The Telescope That Never Sleeps," *Astronomy* (August 1987): 15–20; Anthony C. S. Readhead, "Radio Astronomy by Very-Long-Baseline-Interferometry," *Scientific American* 246 (June 1982), 52–61.

9. Philip Morrison and Phylis Morrison, and the Office of Ray Eames, *Powers of Ten* (New York: Scientific American Books, 1982).

10. N.R.A.O., *The Very Large Array,* 7; J. S. Hey, *The Radio Universe,* 3d ed. (Oxford: Pergamon Press, 1983).

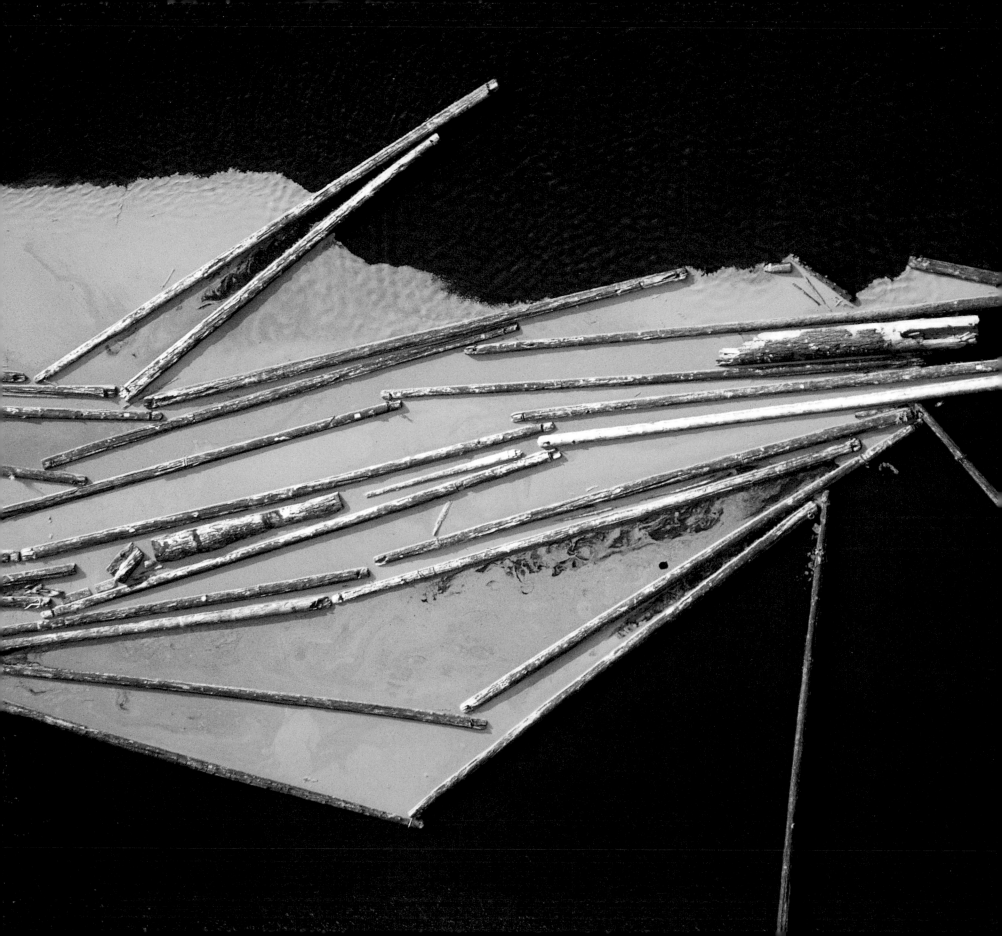

CONTRIBUTORS

James Corner is a landscape architect and associate professor of landscape architecture at the Graduate School of Fine Arts, University of Pennsylvania. He has published a series of articles on landscape-architectural design and theory in a number of international journals and magazines.

Alex S. MacLean, pilot and aerial photographer, founded his own company, Landslides, Inc., in Boston in 1979. His work has been published in *Look at the Land: Aerial Reflections on America,* with essays by Bill McKibben (New York: Rizzoli, 1993).

Denis Cosgrove, professor of geography at the Royal Holloway and Bedford New College, London, is the author of numerous books, most recently *The Palladian Landscape: Geographical Change and Its Cultural Representations in Sixteenth-Century Italy* (State College: Pennsylvania State University Press, 1993).

Michael Van Valkenburgh, landscape architect and professor and chairman of landscape architecture at the Graduate School of Design, Harvard University, has recently published his built work in *Design with the Land: The Landscape Architecture of Michael Van Valkenburgh* (Princeton: Princeton Architectural Press, 1995).

Detail; plate 50.

INDEX

longitude, 5, 56–57. *See* correction lines

long-lots, 7, 17, 31, 62–63

Louisiana, 17, 62–63

Magellan, Ferdinand, 5

Maps. *See* representation; United States Geological Survey

Massachusetts: Brockton, 38–39; Charlestown, 105

mathesis, xvii

McHarg, Ian, 16

Mead, Lake, 73

Measures: numerical, xvii, 5, 28; traditional, xvii, 27, 175*n*7; defined, xvii–xix; modern, xvii–xix, 25, 27–31; ethical, xviii, 26, 30, 33, 34, 36–37, 149; symbolic, xviii, 27, 149; instrumental, xviii, 36–37, 69; and representation, xviii–xix; and cartography, 5; and geometry, 5; and landscape, 25–26, 41; and circumstance, 27, 33, 121; and poetry, 34. *See also* fittingness; geometry; technology

Mesa Verde. *See* Colorado

meter, 28, 177*n*7

military landscapes, 11, 96, 99, 176*n*16

Minnesota: Minneapolis, 102, 106, 174

Mississippi River, 7, 62–63, 124–155

Missouri: Ironton, 47

Missouri River, 81

Mojave Desert, 64–65, 86–87

Montana: Teton River, 93; Havre, 124; Shelby, 126; Chester area, 126–127; Cutbank, 128–129

Mounds, 154–155

National Land Survey, 8–9, 16, 30–31, 36, 41, 45–57. *See also* correction lines; Jefferson, Thomas

Navaho spring-line fields, 138–139

Nevada, 73, 88

New Deal, 9–10

New Mexico: Magdalena, 11, 32, 168–173; Farmington, 89; San Juan Basin, 92; Acoma

Pueblo, 146–147; Pueblo Bonito, 161–164; Chaco Canyon, 161–167

North Carolina: Chapel Hill, viii

North Dakota: Fargo area, 45; Castleton, 50–51, 54, 56; Reynolds, 52; Munich, 118–119

Ohio, 114

Oklahoma, 4

overplowing, 137

Ozark Mountains, 47

Palouse. *See* Washington

Pennsylvania: Lykens, 60–61; Lancaster County, 115, 136

photographs. *See* representation

planning, 4, 15, 32, 37

practical wisdom, 36

Ptolemy, 5

Pueblos, 3, 146–147, 161–164

radio telescopes. *See* Very Large Array

railroads, 9, 54–55, 106–107

rangs. *See* long-lots

rectangular survey system. *See* National Land Survey

representation: aerial, xi, 3–5, 10, 15–18, 175*n*1; photographs, xv–xvi, 175*n*4; map-notation drawings, xvii; maps, xvii, 7, 17–19; and measure, xviii–xix; and landscape, 3, 15–19, 21, 36. *See also* geometry; measures

revetments, 81

Rhode Island: Westerley, 43, 117

rice fields, 111

salination, 75

Savannah River, xx–xxi

scaling, 171

sections, 31, 46, 48

settlement ponds, xx–xxi

shadows, 140–145, 165–167

Smith, John, 7

Snake River, 9, 110

soil conservation, 52–53; 130–137

solar furnace, 79

solar geometry, 6, 141, 158, 163–164, 167

solar orientation, 140–147, 178*nn*3,4

South Carolina, 108

space, 3–7

spacing, 33

spring-lines, 138–141

standardization, 28, 32

stone walls, 43

strip farming. *See* contour farming

sublime, 7, 8, 21, 69

technology, xviii, xix, 36–37; 69. *See also* measures

telegraph, 9

temperance, 36

Tennessee Valley Project, 10

thermal radiation, 139–141, 147

time, 6–8, 158; seasonal, 141, 147. *See also* calendars

townships, 31, 46, 48, 56

train turning circles, 106

transmission lines, 23, 78

Turner, Frederick Jackson, 3

United States Geological Survey, xvii, 7, 8, 175*n*5

Very Large Array Radio Telescope, 11, 24, 149, 168–173, 179*nn*8,10

Walpi. *See* Hopi villages

Washington: Bellingham, 94; Longview, 95, 180; Palouse area, 130, 133–135

West, the, 11–13

wheat farming. *See* dry farming

Whitman, Walt, 3

wilderness, 10

windmills, 13, 82–87

woodlots, 13

CREDITS

All photographs except those listed below are by Alex MacLean.

Photograph on page 14 and plates 40, 91, 92, 93, 94, 109, 110, 114, 115, and 119 are by James Corner.

All drawings are by James Corner.

Most maps are photographically copied from United States Geological Survey (U.S.G.S.) maps.

Most satellite images were taken from *Atlas of North America: Space-Age Portrait of a Continent* (Washington, D.C.: National Geographic Society, 1985).

Drawing, page 32: Plan provided by the National Radio Astronomy Observatory at the Very Large Array, Socorro, New Mexico.

Plate 4: Adapted from Hildegard Binder Johnson, *Order upon the Land* (New York: Oxford University Press, 1976), 77.

Plate 5: Overlaid upon photographic reversal of U.S.G.S. map of Ironton, Missouri.

Plate 6: Adapted in part from Johnson, *Order upon the Land*, 62–63.

Plate 7: Adapted in part from Johnson, *Order upon the Land*, 142.

Plate 15: Adapted from Johnson, *Order upon the Land*, 58.

Plate 55: Dimensioned plan copied from Robert T. Packard, ed., *Architectural Graphic Standards*, 7th ed. (New York: Wiley and Sons, 1981), 34.

Plate 57: The markings across this construction site were part of an art installation called "Drawing on Site," by Sheila Kennedy, Frano Violich, and Matthew VanderBorgh, Boston, 1990.

Plate 90: Plan adapted from Ralph Knowles, *Energy and Form: An Ecological Approach to Urban Form* (Cambridge: MIT Press, 1974), 22.

Plate 96: Plan adapted from Knowles, *Energy and Form*, 28.

Plate 105: Partial images of Walpi Village cut from postcards, produced by Secakuku Enterprises, Hopi Cultural Center, with Beautyway, Flagstaff, Arizona; original photographs by Ben Wittick and John K. Hillers. Plan adapted from Stanley Stubbs, *A Bird's-Eye View of the Pueblos* (Norman: University of Oklahoma Press, 1950).

Plate 108: Plan adapted from Neil M. Judd, *The Architecture of Pueblo Bonito* (Washington, D.C.: Smithsonian Institution, 1964), 4.

Plate 113: Adapted from A. Sofaer, A. V. Zinser, and R. M. Sinclair, "A Unique Solar Marking Construct," *Science* 206 (1979): 283–91; and A. Sofaer, R. M. Sinclair, and L. E. Doggett, "Lunar Markings on Fajada Butte, Chaco Canyon, New Mexico," in *Archaeoastronomy in the New World*, edited by A. F. Aveni (Cambridge: Cambridge University Press, 1982), 169–81.

Plate 117: Plan provided by the National Radio Astronomy Observatory at the Very Large Array, New Mexico.

Plate 118: The survey scan of the northern sky was observed and made by J. J. Condon and J. J. Broderick, National Radio Astronomy Observatory. The bubble-chamber image was made by Cosmotron at Brookhaven National Laboratory.